Say Only Enough

Eddie Williams

Clink
Street

Published by Clink Street Publishing 2021

Copyright © 2021

First edition.

ISBN:
978-1-914498-11-4 - paperback
978-1-914498-12-1 - ebook

ACKNOWLEDGEMENTS

In memory of Jack Donnelly without whom, this book could not have been written.

I would like to offer my thanks to the following:

Pete Guttridge. For his encouragement at the beginning, which has now been rewarded.

Brian Evans. For his support and endorsement, which were instrumental to have the book published.

Julian Donnelly. For his suggestions and corrections, which were necessary.

Prologue

I started to write this book as memories of my working life for my grandchildren, who may, in later years, wonder what their papa did to make his millions. Well not quite. I found I enjoyed writing it and what was intended as a few pages in a folder metamorphosed into what is before you. It was never intended to be the panacea of how to form or succeed in business I do not have the authority for that. There are many authoritative books and biographies written on that subject by people of great proven success. This hopefully offers a different take, of how an average Joe with no entrepreneurial inclinations or ambitions succeeded in forming a business that is still successfully operating today after forty years. It is of someone who was far removed from the single mindedness of a true entrepreneur who is driven with ambition, purpose, motivation, and vision to name but a few. It is of someone born more with a philosophy of wet your finger and stick it in the air.

I offer a brief synopsis. I was born in 1943 in the fair town of Bolton, an only one to loving and supportive parents. We had quite a large extended family of aunts, uncles and cousins. I was married in 1968 and still share that status after fifty-three years with my loving (who still puts up with me) wife Gwen. Our eldest son Michael was born in 1970. Tragically he died from an accident in 1994. His short but very full and meaningful life is still celebrated by his many friends who still provide us with great support. Mark our youngest son was born in1973. He now lives very successfully in Poland having moved there in 2008 with his lovely wife Ania and their three wonderful children Lucas, Megan and Loren.

And there you have it my life described in 266 words, gripping. Hopefully my working life is a little more interesting, well you can find out.

CHAPTER ONE

The Formative Years

'What do you want to do when you leave school?' asked my father, God what a question.

'Can I finish my chips?' I hadn't even given it a thought. Did that mean I had to take some responsibility and do some work? Think of something. 'I wouldn't mind being a rep like you,' was the quickest reply I could think of.

My dad was a representative or salesman for Mrs Twistles self-raising flour. Yes Mrs Twistles! Selling a product with a name like that you had to be good or crazy. As far as I was aware, he spent his days walking from shop to shop and talking. I could manage that. He would walk for miles in pursuit of his job. Eureka! He saw the light decided petrol was cheaper than shoe leather and bought a car (the job gets more appealing). A car, if that's what you could call it. I certainly couldn't brag he'd got a Jag. It had somehow more oil on the inside of the car than in the engine. You didn't sit on the seats you slid off them.

Although still at school, I had an interest in my Dad's job, not just because it kept food in my mouth. I was aware he was a dedicated and hardworking man, who I assessed through listening to his conversations he was good at his job. The nature of the job the freedom it appeared to offer. Not having a set routine every day, being in a way your own boss, percolated into my brain. I presumed the financial rewards at Mrs Twistles however did not match the rising capability of the flour. So, he sought pastures new, where his ability hopefully would be rewarded .One thing about being a salesman, as against many other jobs, is that your ability is obvious, you're either good or not, you have nowhere to hide. You either sell or you don't, your capability is easily defined.

He left Mrs T's and joined R. Green and Co, wine and spirit merchants and bottlers. Bottlers were companies, who surprisingly bottled beer for the large brewers. They could sell this in their own right, to pubs and clubs, or anybody else who might have an inclination to sell or retail the stuff.

One notable event occurred quite early in his new job. One that will always be a first and could be therefore never repeated. He obtained the order to supply the drink to the first nightclub to be opened in Bolton. The opening of this had created much opposition from the anti-goodtime brigade, all other miserable sods and the police. My folks were duly invited to the opening night and took with them another couple Wyn and Alf Entwistle. On arrival, they had been warned by the owner that should drinking continue alter closing time (who would ever think of doing such a thing?) and should they be raided, they must pour their drinks on the floor, bugger the oilcloth.

Sure enough, what a surprise, they were raided. The police, like Custer, determined to make a stand. My dad and Alf had gone to the gents, and guess what, theirs were the only glasses still standing. Why my mother, or her friend, never poured them away is still being investigated. They were charged. Alf had a good position at the town hall (well for the time being). This was not the type of job in the early sixties were being charged with drinking, after hours, in premises that were highly contentious, debauched, and would lead to total damnation, led to automatic promotion. Well, what a surprise, Alf's case was never brought to court (it's not what you know) my dad's was. He was duly charged with drinking after hours. The first prosecution ever brought for drinking after hours in a night club in Bolton. Well after the tickertape parade through the town, he put a notch on his belt, entered the events in his CV and gave up drinking – well on Wednesdays.

My dad, when I was young, had a fascination with second-hand merchandise and it's not because he could always sell it (it's in the blood).It was often because he could fettle it, a northern expression meaning to repair it, restore it, or improve it. He would often come home with stuff he'd bought from some second-hand shop; sometimes good, sometimes not. He would bring things he had won at the local fair (if he could spend time at the fair, the job's getting even better). These would be pots or figurines which he then would spend time painting, the more naff the better, or as my mother would say, 'tarting them up', which made them even worse. Actually, he was very good at art he had great appreciation of it. Which is a little contradictory considering some of the priceless wonders he brought home. I still have one of the paintings displayed in my house and I may say a very good one, which he came home with whilst selling Mrs Twistles self-raising flour.

I digress, my desire to be a rep, well not my desire, the only thing I could think of, I conveyed to my teachers, when we had a session discussing careers. This flummoxed them. It was certainly not on the list of usual jobs. My school was Brownlow Fold Secondary Modern. Modern was pushing it a bit, considering it was built around 1890. This is best described as a good solid Victorian edifice for the sons of gentle folk. Well, gentle was also pushing it. It was known as 'Fout college of Knowledge and Technology'. Fout being a Lancashire expression for fold, a fold being an enclosure for sheep. The last time sheep were in these parts, Cromwell was knocking things about a bit. The knowledge that was imparted was the survival of life, mainly your own, and the technology was pre-clockwork. But l enjoyed it. A job was what you got hopefully on leaving; a career was, well what the hell was it? I can't recall the word being mentioned.

The teachers, on looking back seemed pretty capable. If you had the ability and the desire to learn, the quality of teaching was acceptable. Having failed the eleven-plus and if you were what was determined as a late starter, you could still be transferred to a grammar school, so all is not lost. I'm still waiting for my letter.

What I think was lacking was vision and expectation. It was accepted that you would finish up in painting and decorating, car repairing, welding, bricklaying or some manual job. Not that there is anything wrong with any of these trades; and where would we be without them? But vision and things beyond the normal was in short supply. I have known a number of lads who have made great success of their trades and their own businesses, so it is not a barrier to all, but they are the ones who would not accept the normal.

Academically I didn't shine, more a dull luster. I always managed to stay in the top grade but had a tendency to hover around the bottom. Well, it was hard work and a long way to get to the top. I worked on the theory to just do enough – don't strain yourself. I have never had ambition to achieve or be the top, but on the other hand, I never wanted to fail or be beaten. Just do enough and you'll get through. I must say the theory has been tested over the years and at times I have stepped outside it when, needs must, but I can say they were happy days.

The school had a reputation for being tough. The rumoured initiation for new boys was to be thrown down the cellar steps, and that was just by the teachers. The lads were from hard working-class backgrounds. They were good lads, oh yes, there were fights but they were arranged and promoted. Word got around. There's a scrap in such-in-such back street, between 'Frank the Fist' and 'Billy the Boot' or whoever – spread the word. 'You bring the chairs I'll bring the stretcher.' Sales and promotion were in my blood! I find it surprising and perhaps interesting for those interested in social history. There were many who could be described as hard cases, but I was never aware of any bullying or intimidation, other than by one boy. It's interesting how you hear of bullying in public schools and indeed the then grammar schools. These were mainly, but not all, lads from moneyed or more privileged backgrounds. Yet lads from the other end of the spectrum, where life was certainly not privileged fought their own size or those of equal capability, something for the lefties or sociologists to consider.

You might wonder why I prattle on about events before my sales career and not directly connected to it. Well, they say the formative years make the man in his many forms. Some have more structured upbringings, stricter, high expectations, wealthier, poorer, harder. But you finish up in adulthood formed as you are, never really to change, even if you wanted to. So, I enunciate some of the building blocks which will eventually make the final structure.

One lad who I did scrap with and was friendly with, well most of the time, went to Fout and lived at the end of our row. Originally the skirmishes, if I recall, were pretty equal but in time his extra two stone and strength of a gorilla had somehow a profound effect on his ability to win. Sod this for a game of fairies, said I, if you want a scrap, catch me. To my advantage his extra two stone had the adverse effect on his running ability. Dave was a nice guy and certainly not a bully. His size certainly gave him an advantage over us smaller mortals.

One of our pastimes was the rolling of car tyres. We rolled these with great pride and skill through the streets, Dave with a car tyre never, a bus tyre for him. A gang of us would go to Tootals Park or Toots Park as it was better known. This was more a semi grass playground not exactly Hyde Park. At the far end it rose in a flat-topped hill which, when you climbed to the top, sloped steeply away down to the busy ring road, a hundred foot below. We would stand on the crest strung out like Indians waiting to attack a wagon train. Instead of horses we sat on tyres (imagination is a wonderful thing).

On one of our outings, Geronimo decided to unleash his secret weapon giving one mighty push to his bus tyre. I don't know what velocity a bus tyre travels down a hundred-foot steep slope, but it doesn't hang about. It would hit some undulation, career in the air, crash back to earth, believe me you could stop a tsunami before this. It crossed the near carriage way over the central reservation, across the far carriage way and through the fence of a house backing onto the road. Where it stopped and what further carnage it made was lost to us, the consequences of this could have been very serious. God knows what would have happened if it had hit a car. 'Let's get the hell out of here before the cavalry turn up.' We scarpered minus one bus tyre. What do you learn from this? Never trust an Indian with a bus tyre.

In later years his size found him a job as a bouncer and unfortunately, due to the nature of the job, in one incident he was charged with GBH. The charge was for holding a man under his arm and putting him through a glass door. A trick thank-goodness he never tried on me. In later years he became the landlord of a hard Bolton town-centre pub. I hadn't seen him for possibly twenty-five years until one day I happened to call, as you do, at a nice pub on the outskirts of town and low and behold there's Dave behind the bar.

'Good to see you,' he greets me, as friendly as ever. The guy he shoved through the glass door must have deserved it.

'The last time I saw you, you were in the Nags Head,' I said.

'Yes, you're right.'

'How come you left?' I enquired.

'Well let's put it this way,' he says, 'I was fed up of having no skin on my knuckles.' A great analogy, but I could still beat him at running.

On the subject of running, it's one thing I was quite good at. Well, if you're not so good at fighting make sure you're good at running. How that was going to help me in my sales career I hadn't got a clue. I won the school athletics championship in 1958. I was the best at keeping the egg on the spoon. My prize was a small (it came with a magnifying glass) trophy in hardwood. It measured in height four inches by three with a wooden base. The school crest was displayed with my name, year and the achievement. The big thrill of winning it was not the winning but being presented with it on the school's speech day by none other than Nat Lofthouse, the Bolton Wanderers and England centre forward and one of the greatest of all time. Thirty-one caps for England and twenty-nine goals beat that. I never washed my right hand after for three weeks. In later years my trophy was lost in the trophy cabinet of my sons.

It now has the same minor position within the trophies of my grandchildren.

It was made by 'Atomic Alvin,' the woodwork master who for some reason would insist on his real name of Tommy Calvin. He was the first person who introduced me to a joint, albeit a mortise and tenon. We used to ask: 'Can we have the glue pot on sir?' The last thing we had on our mind was gluing something, and after we had hovered over the glue pot for five minutes, that really was the last thing on our mind. He used to have a regular habit of losing his glasses, well they weren't really lost, more misplaced. They were perched on the top of his head for all to see. He would shout out at the top of his voice: 'Has anyone seen my glasses?' Nobody would say a thing. They would eventually drop down on his nose. It never seemed to occur to him everybody knew. Always remember what you see clearly others may not and use the clarity to your advantage.

Now, you may be wondering, and well you might, what the hell has all this blather got to do with a sales career – and a reasonably successful one at that. I'd have you know nothing, other than to offer a snippet of the formative years which throughout history have been the forming of all great men. Look at Alexander the Great, Napoleon, Wellington, Nelson. To be included in that bunch is a great honour and privilege. So there, now you know. Stay around the first step on the ladder to my chosen career is getting close, but before that, one last life forming incident at 'Four'. The moral being, pay attention, and never indicate, especially when selling, that you know what you're talking about when you don't. Yes, well that went for a Burton a long time ago.

Crotchet Crowther was the music teacher. His outstanding feature was his Beethoven hairstyle. Whether this was intentional, coincidental or meant to impress, it didn't. The guy had a hard time. Trying to teach appreciation of Bach and Mozart when the opposing team was Presley, Little Richard and Buddy Holly was an uphill task of monumental proportions. Considering that half the class, thought that Bach came from a tree and Handel was what you found on a door.

One lesson he had spent half an hour teaching sharps and flats. 'Hindle,' he shouts, 'Come out here and draw a flat on the board.' Hindle, who was certainly no Mozart groupie goes to the board, picks up a piece of chalk and draws what is obviously a house with a chimney and smoke coming out. Crotchet, who watches him do this for twenty or so seconds, never stops him, just stands there speechless. In the meantime, the class is in total disarray, while Hindle is stood there with not a clue, wondering what the hell's going on. Crochet, poor guy, his confidence shattered, was never the same again, he left shortly after. His leaving was referred to as Crowther's last movement.

We had open days, when your parents met the teachers to find out where in the stratosphere their little darling had risen. My mum and dad, for some reason had a meeting with Mr Noakes the headmaster. They must have been worried god knows why; I was quite happy. Anyway, they told me after he'd said the usual script, I summarise:

'He's not the brightest in the class and he could try harder,' what a surprise – 'but he is a very good mixer.' He'd obviously seen me handling the sand and cement in the building skills class. Allow me to digress for a moment and skip sixty-three years. I was recently looking at the deeds of our house which we moved into three years ago. It is in a road of twenty detached bungalows. There is one detached house. Reading the deeds this house was built in 1962 two years before all the others. I noticed it was built by a Mr A Noakes a headmaster. Well, well did you ever. I can imagine his reaction, 'Williams! you finish up being a neighbour of mine, never.'

On the point I mentioned earlier, on the lack of expectation of pupils and the narrowness of the jobs usually considered, there are, as in all things, exceptions. A few years ago, there was an article in the *Bolton Evening News* about an ex-pupil (after my time) who had just become the top insurance salesman in the USA – some achievement. It proves there should be no boundaries. I'm pretty sure he'd have known who Bach and Handel were.

'The time has come,' the Walrus said, 'to think of other things.' The other things being work in my case. If it hadn't come just yet, it was fast approaching. Do I get a job? Applying for a sales manager seemed a bit premature. How about continuing my education at some far-flung establishment? I could find a course on how to become a salesman in three easy lessons. After all, my teachers had said that if I would apply myself, work a bit harder, I was quite capable of going places, unfortunately they never mentioned which places.

I know, how about Bolton Tech'? It's only twenty minutes on the bus to there. Let's have a gander. Here's a course they do: 'A Commercial and Business Course.' That should help me onto my first million. Now let's see what it includes. Bookkeeping, well I'm not particularly interested in betting, if that's what it's about. Shorthand, that could be handy, I could spell just as I wanted, and nobody would know the difference. English, 'to be or' whatever it is. I presume that could come in handy. After all, I'd 'ave to speak right proper in my selling career. Well look at that, Business Studies and Marketing, just the ticket. Marketing is something to do with selling, isn't it? Sign me up.

If first impressions are important, I sure made one on the first day of my further education. I entered the classroom as directed and sat by the first desk by the door, which was one of the few still vacant. I chatted to the guy next to me and we perhaps waited ten minutes, when the door burst open as though hit by a battering ram. In strides the teacher, travelling at a similar velocity as a runaway bus tyre.

I was sitting with my legs extended beyond the front of the desk. He, the teacher, looking straight ahead did not notice the two appendages so positioned as to impede his progress – and they did. Upon contact his forward trajectory took on an angle of sixty degrees his head therefore being far more forward than his feet. His considerable progress was arrested by the kind intervention of the front desk, which he grabbed, as you would a life buoy in similar desperate circumstances. He waited a few seconds, to regain what modicum of composure he could muster, and turned with the expression of who the hell caused that? The offending obstructions had of course, been duly retracted to their proper housing, and little Lord Fauntleroy sat there with the innocent expression of 'not me guv'.

In the absence of a block of concrete, Sherlock came to the elementary conclusion that feet must have been the culprit. The two obvious suspects – sorry, guilty – well one was, were those two by the door. 'Would you keep your feet under your desk please at all times?' was his retort, and the laser penetration and direction of his eyes left no doubt as to where one of the guilty ones sat. Do I admit to it and apologise? Well, he never asked for an admission – stand your ground! Being a generous person, and also one who always admits when he's wrong, yes well (don't tell my wife) I thought I'd share the responsibility with my co-suspect. Well, if I'm here for a year you have got to work together. The teacher interrupted my thoughts. 'There are two classes on the course and the other has three lads in it. Would any of you here like to go into that one to even up the numbers?' My hand shot up. Don't spend time considering, let's start afresh thought I. How you can start afresh when you haven't started anything is perhaps a little premature. He accepted my volunteering readily. Happy perhaps, along with my co-suspect, to be rid of one of the little shits who had made his introduction so memorable.

The lack of maturity of my tender years was insufficient for me to realise, that owning up to a mistake or misdemeanour, especially when not requested to do so, acquired your brownie points in trust and respect that far outweighed the indignity of a big bollocking – oh, sorry, chastisement.

My academic business career began. The first steps to an empire I never even gave a thought to. My decision to move class proved right. There were four lads and just sweet sixteen girls. The lads were a good bunch, and we became good mates. I am still friends with one, both of us now living in the same village.

It was interesting being in a mixed class, especially coming from an all-boys' school. I only really fancied one girl, who sat in the desk behind. We did have a small dalliance, which I wanted to exchange for a bigger one. Unfortunately, the minimal endured. She was going out with a butcher and he would sometimes meet her after class. It was the meat cleaver he carried around which somehow dampened my ardour. The romance never really developed beyond good friends. Who knows, if it hadn't been for butcher boy.

The dominance of girls was not so much a distraction as competition. After all, who wanted to be beaten by a girl? And there lies a tale. The bookkeeping part of the course was, what could one say, riveting – no! I couldn't credit anything to it. Shorthand, if you found squiggles fascinating, this is your forte. English, well I spoke it, didn't I? Well, in a fashion. Business studies, moderate. Marketing eureka! I've found my home.

The culmination of our new-found knowledge came to a climax about a month before the course ended. The class would be divided into five groups, four groups of four girls, and one of the four lads. A competition would be held, and each group would be given a product which they would market and promote just as an advertising and marketing agency would do. The winner would be, in the eyes of the teachers, the one who made the finest presentation. Oh boy, this is for me. If I am to make a career in sales, the opportunity to prove I am a sales and marketing prodigy is in my lap.

The five groups assembled to be given some 'do's' but mainly 'don'ts' allowed in our presentation and the products we each had to market. Each group was categorised by letter A, B, C, D, and E. We were group E – well women and women first. The products were read out. The ones I can remember were: a raincoat, sun cream, a toothbrush, and two others. And guess what we drew? The soddin' toothbrush! Bridget Bardot is photographed in a raincoat with a tight belt to show more curves than an hourglass. You could imagine a picture of some leggy blonde on some exotic beach, smothering herself in sun cream, looking greasier than a chip pan. What have we got? the picture of someone's gob! Still my boy, you're the man – well not quite yet.

The lads suggested me as leader or front man. More to do with my enthusiasm than any perception they had of my marketing ability. The others chose theirs to head their team. The sun cream Brigade Group B was led by Queen Vic (yes even that pub was named after her). Her name was Victoria and she acted in the manner of a Queen. She spoke with a plum in her mouth (that's a Bolton plum) and surprisingly she was not on my twenty-first birthday party list. Well, little does she know, she's going to be dethroned. We had two weeks to plan our task. We were allowed time in the day and I put time in at night. Is this what's called homework? I don't think any of the other lads did any night shift, so I think it's fair to say I contributed the most. But input they certainly had.

'The first thing we need is a name,' I suggested. What did we come up with? 'Wrigley's, The Wrigley Toothbrush.' Hmm, yes well, perhaps looking back it…Well, it was a well-known name. The product associated with it had association with the mouth and it brought a fresh clean taste, like our toothbrush (that's if it's not chewed for too long). That's the spearmint, not the toothbrush.

'Why don't we use the word "turbo" in the name?' Rod suggested.

'What the hell's turbo?' was the unanimous reply.

'It's a new thing I've read; it increases speed and performance in cars.'

'What's that got to do with a toothbrush?'

'We call it the "Wrigley Turbo Toothbrush" – it's new, it's modern, it's fast.'

'Well, it's certainly a mouth full'

'Funny'

'People wouldn't understand turbo.'

'They will soon, I bet.'

'Ok, let's give it a go; it's different.' We all agreed.

We did the design, we did the description, why to use, when to use, how to use, where to use. In fact, we ran out of uses. We had bullet points by the score, all promoting its advantages, benefits, design, and availability. The only thing missing was a slogan. I insisted how important this was for product association. Oh yes, I'd been reading. Doesn't everyone know 'Hoover beats as It sweeps as it cleans?'

Well, the Day of Judgment came. We assembled our displays. Ours stood out like a beacon, shining, glittering, colourful. Well, we thought so, and we weren't biased.

We eyed the opposition, well moderate, good try. We stood by our displays and the arbiters came in. We were the third in line. They spent around five minutes with each display asking questions, making notes. They spoke quietly to each group, cunning devils. The one thing we forgot was learning to lip read. We're next. 'Good afternoon.' 'An excellent display and presentation.' they offered. Liking how we had shown the best technique for good brushing and how a Wrigley Toothbrush would complement this very initiative. They liked the punch the presentation gave, and how the mock advert we had designed arrested your attention. They were done they moved on, we felt pleased. We watched if they spent more time with any particular group. Without having a stopwatch all seemed fair. They left immediately after seeing the last group and said they would be back in half an hour with their decision. We all went to the refectory for a drink, all staying in our little groups the tension getting to us.

We were back in good time, awaiting those who held the embryo of my future in their hands. They came, they'd seen, they'd compared. 'Well may we say,' began the head of business studies, 'what an excellent job you have all made of this rather testing exercise.'

And so he continued with the plaudits for another three hours, or so it seemed. Get on with it, just give us our prize.

'The decision has been hard and very close. I will start with the second prize, and this goes to Group E for the Wrigley Toothbrush. 'WHAT?! Hold me back lads, while I get at him. Oh no, it can't be, don't tell me: 'The winner is by a narrow margin, Group B Sunten. That little pimple faced, bogeyed, bowlegged, boring, flat chested little tart. Not that I hold a grudge, in any way, anyone but her.

We stood there comatose not saying a thing. They spent a few moments with the newly crowned monarch, and then they made their way over to the King in exile.

'We are very sorry boys, but they just pipped you. It was a very hard and close decision. Your presentation had many facets superior to theirs (I must look up the word 'facet'). But it really was their name and slogan which clinched it. 'Sunten is a very catchy play on words it rolls off the tongue. And their slogan complemented it. "Sunten, The Cream of The Beach". Your slogan "In a Rush then Clean Your Teeth with a Turbo Brush", did, may I say, not quite have the same ring to it, but very well done in all other aspects.'

I knew we had not concentrated enough on the slogan. Grudgingly, I accepted they were right; product association is what we lacked. Well, we all know 'it does what it says on the tin' well, we didn't. You should never totally lose. Use a defeat in a positive way, learn from it .The real world was fast approaching, and so to hell with academia. I need a job do they need me? Of course they do.

CHAPTER TWO

The First Step

Nine months was the incubation time for my first job. It takes nine months from conception to birth and there the similarity ends. I joined a large regional T.V. Hi-Fi and Radio retailer as an assistant trainee salesman. Well, television was the new wonder, and now fast expanding into the mass market. The future looked bright.

There was one element that was abundant very soon, 'Boredom.' The training was intensive. It took me a month to master turning on and turning off a set. Well, come on, there were a number of different sets and the knobs were in different places. After I'd mastered this it became easier. The changing of channels BBC to ITV I sailed through in two weeks. And then the most complex was left to the last. Contrast, Brightness, Vertical Hold and the pinnacle – Horizontal Hold cracked it – where's my certificate? Not until you've mastered radios.

I'd heard about this. That meant tuning in by twiddling knobs to the Light Programme or the Home Service, with the occasional foray into Radio Luxembourg (you little devil, that's illegal). No, sorry, that's Radio Caroline. This proved a piece of cake. Only one thing left: oh my God, Hi-Fi. This is now getting serious and indeed it could be. People seemed to take this and the newer development, stereo, very seriously and personally. Being sensitive to any background noise and receptive and critical of the total sound and reproduction was the 'in thing' demanding a reproduction 'as if you were there,' wherever there was. It did require more knowledge, skill, and input than the 'goggle box' or 'cat's whisker'.

Having an interest, or a bent, for Hi-Fi, however, did not, in my mind, make up for the total boredom of waiting for customers to appear and then, when they did, having one of the senior staff invariably nick them.

Three of us, of similar age, had started around the same time. Luckily, due to the rebuilding of the store just prior to us joining, an imaginative architect had incorporated into the new design a B.R.A.F. – 'A Boredom Relief Assisted Feature.' These were two large glass doors which were the main entrance to the store. They were, if I recall, quite unique for the time – doors of that type only just beginning to come into fashion. The three of us would stand chatting, waiting for the 'three times a week' big bang. And this wasn't just a theory but a fact.

Due to the unfamiliarity of these types of doors and the undoubted clarity of the glass, the unsuspecting customer would walk into them. Instead of rushing to offer sympathy and assistance, we would wait to see the reaction of the slightly concussed bewildered, and what was, two seconds previously, potential customer. If we had really thought this through we could have laid bets on which days, what time of day, how many per day. That would not just have further relieved the boredom, it would have made the event meaningful worthwhile and profitable. Profitable being appropriate as the company name was Proffitts'.

This weekly occurrence came to a head, no pun intended, on a very wet and rainy day. We were in our usual grandstand position, in good view of the door, when we observed a man running down the pavement obviously trying to get out of the rain. The doors were positioned in a large alcove at right angles to the street. On reaching the alcove, he veered left and ran straight into the doors. This was the big bang. His face was flat against the glass and his nose bent to one side. His lips were pressed tight to the glass as though kissing it. His arms were spread eagled and he slid down the glass to his knees, like some cartoon character hitting a similar immovable object. Luckily and amazingly, as far as I can recall, the man had no serious injury other than shock. This was very fortunate, as serious injury there could have been. Enough was enough, the powers that be, and not before time, put identification on the doors. And enough was enough for me. You can only take a certain amount of moronic entertainment. It's time to move on.

My financial and accountancy skills – ok, my 'bookkeeping part one' – had lain dormant for nine months. In reality they had never at any time been much awakened. Well, perhaps it's time to stimulate the market. Let's have a look at what's on offer. 'Ha Ha', yes, just the ticket! 'Financial director required for large international engineering company.' Qualification hmm, yes, not a mention of bookkeeping part one. Not to worry, I might not have to aim so high. What's this: 'Accounts trainee required for Paint Manufacturers' must be able to handle a teapot and sweeping brush when required, sounds perfect.

'The Accounts department, that's where you'll be based,' the company secretary informed me at the interview. "Now, have you any experience of handling money"

'Well, I've had spending money since I was ten.'

God knows how I managed to get the job but get it I did. I only found out later, that when I joined, they'd taken out extra insurance for insolvency. I worked as assistant to the chief accounts clerk. As she was the only one and I was the only assistant, you could say I was the deputy accounts clerk. How's that for instant promotion? One of my main functions was to operate a large, ageing comptometer. Now for anyone under fifty, it's an adding, subtracting, dividing, multiplying, button pushing, handle pulling, card inserting, creaking, banging, stomach turning accounting machine. Why they ever got rid of them I'll never know. It was rumoured that Reginald Dixon (who remembers him?) started on one of these, before he progressed to the Mighty Wurlitzer at Blackpool Tower.

But master it I did. I wasn't letting a cold calculating piece of steel, whose 'offspring' calculated how to get men on the moon, get the better of me.

Being the office junior, of course, I was asked if I would make the tea. Haha, hence the requirement to handle a teapot and a brush – and I thought they were joking. Well, I made it for the first and last time on my second day. If they think I'm going to make this every day until someone below me starts, they have another thing coming. I had the power in my grasp to make a good cup, a not so good cup, or a bad cup. Not that I could be quite so skilful. Let's not leave them in any doubt as to my tea making ability. Yes, the sink was where a considerable amount of it went. How dare they tear me away from my beloved Mighty Wurlitzer. A lesson to be learned: if you are invested with the power – use it for the good. Well, it was for the good – who'd want my tea? I was only thinking of them.

I was given the usual rookie initiation in the first week. As well as paint manufacturers', they were specialist oil blenders for the mills. I was asked to go down to the oil shop and ask for a 'snot rag'. Now, I knew perfectly well what a snot rag was, having used one to clear my nose on many occasions. But being innocent, naïve, and mainly stupid I presumed it was some technical terminology or name for something. I approached this large elderly boiler suited gentleman, and said, 'I've been asked to come down for a snot rag.' He looked at me for a couple of seconds and then said in a very calm and nice manner: 'I'm sorry son they're having you on, my names Hankey – they will have their little jokes.'

Being paint manufacturers and oil blenders you were aware of the volatility and indeed combustibility of the works and premises. They were on the A list for fire response. You only had to turn on the gas fire and five fire engines arrived. One of the lads in the laboratory was a member of the Auxiliary Fire Service. He used to tell me of his exploits at weekends of practices and call outs. One thing he did tell me which I wish never to have to put in practice. If ever you are in a building which is on fire and you are groping your way through dense smoked filled corridors with poor visibility. You will probably have your arms outstretched to feel for any obstructions. Always make sure you have the back of your hands facing away from you. The normal or natural way would be to have the palm of your hands facing forward but should any live wire have fallen and be across your path your instinct would be to grab it, and good night Vienna. If the back of your hands touched it, they retract and then you die of smoke inhalation.

Not long after being imparted with this subsection three, paragraph four of the fire safety manual, we had a fire. Don't panic Mr Mainwaring was the call, and we all exited the premises in the manner by which we had never been told how to. We assembled in the street and stood watching as fire engines arrived from all directions. There was no obvious sign of a fire, no flames leaping out of the roofs. I had never seen as many fire appliances in one location. I asked one of the firemen, "With all these fire engines here what happens if you're called to another fire?" "We are covered by other stations in other areas" He answered. I commented "Does that mean it could take longer for them to get there?" "Possibly" he responded. "That's a bit unfortunate for those who have the fire."

"It could be" he said "but in which case we just ask them to keep it going till we get there." This man had missed his way, instead of climbing the ladder he should have been treading the boards.

One of those assembled in the street was of course my friendly Fire Auxiliary Service mate. I thought if there's any problem, he'll sort it. We understood the source was in the oil shop. After an hour or so panic over, and we were allowed to return indoors, a bit of a damp squib. Two or three from the fire brigade stayed around for a few days and were joined occasionally by the police. We presumed they were doing an investigative job, and they certainly were. The result was revealed a couple of weeks later. My Fire Auxiliary friend had been arrested for arson. He was a pyromaniac, and a bad one at that. If he couldn't burn this place down, he should have his membership of the pyromaniac society cancelled. Pyromaniac he may have been, but the tip he gave me has not been forgotten.

The days weeks and months trundled on. I pressed buttons, pulled handles, inserted cards. To offset the boredom,

I sometimes inserted cards, pulled handles and pressed buttons. The variety in this job was amazing. One of the reliefs and freedoms of the day was my job, nay responsibility, to take money and cheques to the bank. I did this at great risk without an armed escort. Well, I could still run a bit. And I had a hard head from repeatedly banging it against a brick wall when I didn't get my own way as a kid – well, "till I was nineteen". The freedom of the half hour, ok three quarters, one hour, maybe one and a half hours. All right, if you insist, two hours. I better pack this in or they'll be sending for the police.

The freedom of the great outdoors was wonderful. Bradshawgate, Deansgate and Great Moor Street. Where else can I go? Mind you, the draw of seeing one of the girls behind the till at the bank helped. She was attractive. Little did I know in two years' time I would get to know her and date her. As well as this great perk with the job, well, you couldn't really call it a perk, but I did. I'd fight anybody who tried to take it off me. Well, if needed I'd call on my old mate Dave I still knew where he lived.

I was friendly with Richard the son of the MD. He was a great guy. He was around fifteen years older than me with a young family. Every so often we would play tennis at lunch times. I'd let him win, of course. The company had four reps, all in their fifties or sixties. They covered an area of Lancashire, Cheshire, and North Wales. I decided to broach the subject. I told him I had always fancied being in sales as a representative and should one retire, or leave, would there be a possibility of me being considered for the vacancy? His reply was very positive. Not a bloody chance.

I am pleased to say he was actually very receptive. He said he would mention it to the company secretary, and his father, and they would discuss it. Should they consider me possibly suitable, it could of course, be sometime before this could happen. I had laid the seed, let us hope it flourishes.

For the foreseeable future I would have to keep pressing the buttons and playing the Mighty Wurlitzer. One memorable event which occurred owing to my working at a paint manufacturers and oil blenders was the re-enactment of a 1200-year-old defence tradition. Now, that's got you guessing. In retrospect, considering I had sewn the seed for a possible future sales career, it may have been a little reckless. But so what? The future was the future – live for now.

The West Lancashire Moors are positioned to the north of Bolton. The most prominent peak on the west side of these is Rivington Pike. It was used over the centuries, to light a beacon to warn of invaders. It was one of the chains throughout the country, before mobile phones put a stop to it. It was easily visible from the coast, being the first hill for thirty miles, one of my mates suggested:

'Why don't we light a beacon on the top like they used to.'

The last time that was used was to warn of 'Bollok the Blood Axe' and his merry band of Viking missionaries.'

What a thought. They have now changed Long Ships to rubber inflatables and the ones on board are seeking sanctuary and refuge, gone are the days of rape and pillage. What a great idea, we all agreed.

'How do we do it?'

'Well, *you* work at a paint place.' Three eyes turned to me.

'So what?'

'You can get the paint.'

'What do we want paint for'

'No, the stuff that goes into paint – It's very burnable isn't it? and that oil you deal in, what more do you need?'

'I'll have to think on this one, I've got a blossoming sales career to think of.'

'I've thought about it, we'll do it.'

I asked discreetly, in the paint shop, if I could have some Pitch. This is an extract from coal and is used in the roofing industry, and more importantly, burns like buggery. Luckily my dad wanted to do the garage roof didn't he? I also acquired a gallon of creosote and turps subs, ideal for ignition. Getting the rags from the oil shop might prove a little more difficult.

These were used for cleaning up oil spillage, and keeping the place generally, oil free. They were totally impregnated with oil. They were quickly disposed of being very combustible unfortunately the wood for the annual communal bonfire behind my folks' house was very wet due to the heavy rain. They would be ideal for lighting the fire. Thank you very much, one more thing. The company used glass carboys for the storage of chemicals and acid. These were housed in a protective steel basket, with a diameter of approximately 70cm and a height of 80cm. One of these baskets would be ideal for housing all the ingredients being strong, light and incombustible. When painted and laid on its side and lined with a padded quilt, it would make an ideal dog basket, wouldn't it?

We obtained from somewhere a rope. This we soaked in the pitch overnight. Having

checked the weather forecasts for the last forty years a Saturday night was decided on. There was more planning in this than D Day. Only one problem, how do we get it there? It's amazing how many campaigns have fallen down in history owing to the most obvious requirement being overlooked. Six years developing the atomic bomb, then they realised they hadn't got a rocket. 'We need an estate car we can't put all this in a boot.'

A lesson to be learned, you can get so embroiled in and enthusiastic about a project, mission, event, whatever you want to call it, you forget a fundamental necessity. Not only does this mean we may have to change dates until we can obtain a vehicle, but a car won't even do. We need an estate or a van. The only person with an estate car was Geoff's dad. 'Sweet talk him Geoff' was our request, and sweet talk his dad he did. Easy for Geoff, who later became a Methodist Minister, guiding his flock on how to live an honest, responsible, law abiding life. The night was good clear and cold but windy. The road to the launch site was not good. It was an earth road undulating with occasional small gullies and potholes. It was drivable slowly but not the type you would choose for a relaxing spin on a November night. The rags had been packed and sealed in various bags they made a large bundle. With the pitch, turps, rope, and metal basket plus two of us in the back it was like a highly volatile sardine tin.

Our destination was about a mile along the side of the moor, to a very dark, isolated, remote and windy location. It took us around twenty minutes to get there to be met with the most unexpected site. There at the bottom of the peak of the hill was parked a car with two indistinguishable persons inside. There had been no cars up here for the last 300 years. And of all the hills, in all the world they had to pick the one we were on. I still find it difficult to understand why a man and a woman would go to all that trouble to drive up there just to listen to the radio and Saturday Night Is Music Night. They were obviously listening to Tina Turner's 'Steamy Windows'. If we were surprised at seeing them, imagine how they were on seeing us, well once they cleared a window. They had picked the most isolated spot they could find for their musical pleasure, when this car arrives with four toss pots with a load of god knows what, which they are now carting up the hill. And cart it up we did to the top.

The wind, it was off the scale, taking full advantage of the lack of obstruction between us and the coast thirty miles away. We placed the basket about ten feet from the castellated tower which dominated the peak of the hill. The oil rags were emptied into the basket. The rope was twined around and placed onto the rags. It was filled to the brim. We poured on the pitch and the turps and stood back. Gordon was the man charged with the ignition; again, a little forethought may have avoided some anxiety. Come on I mean who would ever have thought at a thousand feet on a November night and thirty miles of open plain to the coast before you, it would have been windy.

Matches are not made for a force eight gale. Luckily we had a near full box. We gathered around the basket to form as much protection as we could, eureka we had a flame. We stood there in relief, but not for long. It took what seemed quite a few seconds for the flame to develop. There was a rumble and hissing and then, oh boy did it go, from nothing to full throttle in the blink of an eye. The flame shot eight to nine feet vertically. It was rounded as the shape of the basket and tapered at the top. It was no exaggeration to say it was similar to a rocket engine only this flame had an upward trajectory. It was nearly as high, and it illuminated the stone castellated tower. We stood staring and I think a little shocked at the speed and intensity of the flame. We decide as one to get the hell out of it. We careered down the hill with no safety in mind. The music loving couple had left obviously the music had reached the necessary climax. Had they seen the show, would we ever know?

We made our way back and through the well populated suburb at the base of the moor. It took about twenty minutes and the flame was still very visible, its reflection highlighting the tower. We were jubilant it had been a success and gone just as we had planned. It must have been observed by many as we later found out. I had mentioned to one of the women in the office who lived at the bottom of the moor, to look out on the Saturday night toward the tower. You might find it interesting. It was on the following Thursday she put on my desk the local paper. There in highlighted print on the front page was a headline. 'NASTY PRANK SPOILS FIREMANS BALL.' It read to this effect. On Saturday night a fire was observed on the top of the Pike. The chief officer and his deputy had to leave the annual ball dressed in their dinner suits to attend. On arrival at the scene, they found a burnt-out carboy basket. It went on to express the shock horror and the degenerating social actions of the populous, or something of that nature. They wouldn't have said that if old Bloodaxe had been on his way, very ungrateful.

Now it is feasible that someone in officialdom reading this can recall the event, or perhaps had heard about it. Now with the evidence and admission of the occurrence as described, they may think after fifty-seven years, in some vindictive and tiny minded way, this should not go unpunished. They may be able to bring some trumped-up charge based on some reference to some long-ago case like 'such a body-v-such a body'. But they would require a witness, as I deny any involvement. What if one of our music lovers still annoyed with our interruption spoiling their musical pleasure came forward. They then demanded witness protection, change of identity and address. Even though they had only been in that isolated, remote cold and windy spot innocently listening to Saturday Night Is Music Night. Well, let me tell you, your car registration is safe with me.

CHAPTER THREE

Strike up the Band

I sat one morning, a few months later, in my normal posture at the Mighty Wurlitzer, when Richard came to me and asked if I could come into Mr Roberts' office. He gave no reason. Oh God, have the music lovers reared their head, has my bookkeeping class one not been sufficient to stave off liquidation? I had never been called formally into Mr Roberts' office before. His demeanour seemed relaxed, not like I was due for a sacking. I followed him into the office. There was Mr Roberts, and the company secretary. 'Please have a seat, Eddie,' I sat in what appeared a very relaxed and convivial atmosphere. 'How are you?' asked Mr Roberts' a very gentle and courteous man of the old school. His attitude would be no different if you had just saved the company from financial ruin, or you were being sacked with immediate effect. No clues so far. 'Richard mentioned some time ago you were interested in a rep's position. Well, we have been discussing it for a while, and we are able to offer you one if you are still interested.' Forget a pools win, forget the lottery, this was beyond that. Well perhaps not, but nearly. He continued 'We have moved round some of the areas and hope to expand a little on one of them.' Now don't get tongue-tied in your reply. Not particularly conducive with a rep's job. 'Thank you very much, and I'm certainly very interested.'

He went on to explain what the change of areas were and how the most senior rep had willingly given up some areas to reduce his workload and he was happy for me to spend time with him to hopefully give me the grounding and introduction to some of the customers. He would retain a number of the larger ones, but I was free to call on all the others and of course hopefully get new accounts. The area covered included the Greater Bolton area, a couple of the close towns and North Wales. Oh boy I would have to spend time away. This is almost getting international. I would have a car; all be it a second hand one. Only a second hand one, what type of job is this? Should I push for a new one, hold it boy, don't get ahead of yourself. I willingly accepted and expressed my great appreciation. In retrospect they were taking a risk, all be it a calculated one, as they had known me for a number of years, even so at twenty-one all the other reps were old enough to be my father. Who is this young upstart I could hear their welcome now? I was to start as soon as they could get someone with the same musical ability as myself to play the Mighty Wurlitzer. Hopefully within three weeks.

'Let the drums roll out, let the trumpet call, while I shout out, strike up the band.' So Ira Gershwin said, I couldn't have said it better. I spent time familiarising myself in detail with the products which I knew quite well. I went through the oil shop, the paint shop, the putty shop. Someone was appointed within two weeks; I was to start the following Monday I arrived at work dressed like a million-dollar trooper minus riding boots.

I spent a couple of weeks with my mentor who gave me a crash course and a basic grounding in the art of singing, with a bit of selling thrown in. He was around sixty and had been with the company from a young man. He was very jovial and would suddenly when talking burst into song with his basso profundo voice and continue for a short period whatever he was talking about by singing it. It was like living in an opera. On longer journeys I would get extracts from *Rigoletto* (which he called wriggle your toe), *The Barber of Seville* and god knows what else. It was enjoyable as I did a bit of singing myself (not opera), so we harmonised if not in voice, but in interest. He was a very good rep of the old school. He was friendly and knowledgeable and obviously liked by those we met and that he taught me is the fundamental thing of selling. If you are liked, you are halfway to the order. The other half is a little harder so after two weeks I was up and running, well walking next, I was on my own. I had learnt some of the fundamentals, a delusional 50%. The other 50% I still had to acquire and I got a small percentage of it on the Monday morning of my very first call.

I had been given a list of customers and decided to make my first call on the nearest one. They were well established glass merchants or glaziers, and they bought putty.

Although I tried to appear relaxed and confident, I am sure there were signs in my demeanour which negated this appearance. I asked at reception if I could see Mr Edwards who was the founder of the company. The receptionist phoned him, and I was directed to his office and knocked on the door. 'Come in' was the reply in a strong and authoritative voice. He was a large man and quite a commanding figure. He wore a pinstripe suit and looked more suited to the Chancellor of the Exchequer or the chairman of I.C.I. than the boss of a two-bit glaziers. 'You're new,' he said. God is it so obvious? That undermined my false air of vast experience 'What can I do for you?' he said in a cut-glass voice. I thought for a second I was in the wrong establishment. His accent was upper class Knightsbridge the type that would have described the Rolling Stones like an alternative name to a fence and a town in Middlesex you've got it, the 'Railing Staines' pure Bolton. 'Well, you can give me an order, you pompous pinstriped boss of a putty procurer' was my immediate thought, now remember the customer's always right. Whoever came up with that one had never called here, especially on his first call. 'I wondered if you needed any putty,' I said in what seemed a pathetically week voice. In retrospect it seemed a stupid question to ask to someone who epitomised the Chancellor of the Exchequer. 'We might, I will check,' whereupon he picked up the phone and posed the question to some underling and wrote down the requested items.

Now putty came in tins of varying weights one pound, three pound and upwards. 'Yes, we'll have tin ones, and tin threes' and he continued with a few more items. 'Thank you' I replied. 'How many do you want of the ones and threes?' This seemed to confuse him. He looked at me with the expression of what the hell do you mean. 'Tin he thundered it comes after nine,' he said. 'What does?' said I 'Tin Oh, ten!' I replied. 'Yes tin,' vocalised with an expression of you stupid boy. He was the epitome of a pretentious, putty procurer of pervading pomposity. I presume there's always one.

If being thrown in the deep end makes you swim, I'd managed to get to the side, and deep water didn't seem as frightening. I'm sure being my first call accentuated the experience. But I'd done what I was supposed to do get an order. My record was 100%. It was obviously downhill from here. I am sure the experience was tempered by nerves and eagerness to impress and gain an order. Well on the latter I had succeeded, my footprint for impression is questionable. The main thing gained was experience, you never know who you are going to meet. Just accept whoever or however they are. Just get the order.

One of the great enjoyments of selling or being a representative is meeting people and the diversity of them. You have got as a generality to like people. If on the whole you don't, get out of the job. The job is people. Meeting discussing assessing observing, patience and tolerance are essential. People often assess that a salesman has got to be a good talker a good listener would be more accurate. It is obvious if you want any success you have got to be able to converse and articulate with clarity and in a meaningful way, but the art is saying only enough and no more. This comes with experience. I had a boss who was very likeable and an excellent talker. He would sell the product with ease, but then he would buy it back. He didn't know when to stop.

The initiation was now over I needed a strategy. I would call on and familiarise myself with the existing accounts but would try to open a portfolio of new ones and stake my own claim on them. The customer base was mainly commercial or industrial. Mills using specialist oils, local authorities, builders' merchants, manufacturers, building and plumbing contractors. I would certainly endeavour to open new accounts with these but would also try the retail outlets DIY, Ironmongers, hardware, decorating shops. We supplied very few of these. The problem with them was the smaller quantities they would order and justifying the cost of delivery. The retail outlets proved a success ordering mainly the bituminous paint, putty and creosote. These combined with a few new ones in the traditional customers made for quite an impressive list of new accounts in the first six months. This was well received and commented on by the front office.

Included in my patch was North Wales down to Anglesey with a line across to Stoke-on-Trent and the Potteries. My God this was like going on holiday. Well, I can tell you a rainy November night in Blaenau Ffestiniog is not Barbados and the anticipation of nights away soon wore thin but persist I did, never forgetting my sun cream sorry Sunten. I would be away for a week finishing up in Stoke. I always stayed when in Stoke at the same B&B. Often it was the same guys who were there each time I stayed and we would go out playing darts or to Stoke City at the old Victoria Ground, well you couldn't do that in Barbados. One night I couldn't get in, so I decided after a few pints to sleep in the car, in the car park of the transport café next door. Never again! Cold cramped young and very foolish. Boy did I know how to spend my expenses. At least there was a good breakfast in the café but not a good idea when you have got a full day looking 'spick and span'.

I spent about two years on the road with the company and I think somehow became disillusioned with the job. The same repeated calls, 'Good morning, how are you, do you want anything?' 'Well, it's not a good morning, I'm not very good, and I don't want anything, so sod off!' Not quite like that but you get the drift. The company had been very good to me and I think I gave them a very good return. When I gave my notice in, they tried hard to dissuade me, but I'd made up my mind. I wanted a change perhaps a bigger challenge. Were there any vacancies on the next Everest expedition for a putty salesman, it would be just my luck a double-glazing salesman had got there first.

CHAPTER FOUR

Pastures New

Now this advertisement looks interesting. 'Stand in required for Long John Silver must have one leg and a friendly parrot'; too big a change, on the other hand. 'A vacancy has occurred for a Duplicator and Photocopying engineer [OK technician] with some sales experience,' for a Manchester based Office Equipment Company. Now that's a change, little did I know how different, educational, mind broadening, interesting, career developing and fun it would prove to be.

The company was a leading Manchester Office Equipment Company, supplying and repairing typewriters, adding machines, office furniture, Dictaphones, yes, one of those original letter dictating machines, responsible for the well-known request of a secretary to her boss, 'Can I please use your Dictaphone?''No use your finger like everybody else.' The duplicating and photocopying department or reproduction division as it was aptly known, was newly formed, it had been in operation for about six months. It was headed by a man called Dennis Makin, a great boss and a great character a late forty-year-old Dennis the Menace.

He had been in the reproduction business of various kinds for many years, working and selling Gestetner duplicators which were the market leaders. He was obviously very experienced this was offset by my total inexperience. There was just the two of us in the department, causing no great worry for Gestetner. We sold a duplicator called Rex Rotary manufactured in Holland. The other products we sold were photocopiers. My initial job was to repair maintain and service these and Dennis's was to sell them.

The priority was to familiarise myself with the range, and to find out the workings of them. It was certainly a do it yourself learning experience. There were no training courses (these would come later, on the new electrostatic copiers) There were two types of duplicator, the manual operated by a handle and the electric operated by a simple switch. The mechanics of both were the same. The original type wet copiers with developing fluid were basically a motor, rollers and a light source. I learned some would say the best way, self-taught, trial and error, with the aid of manuals. After two weeks of pulling pushing unscrewing unclipping bolts nuts springs, I was a signed up fully experienced chartered reprographic engineer. Next job the space industry!

The disadvantage of being only two of us and me the only one on the service side, I had nobody to learn from. Dennis was very good he would help where he could, always encouraged and never pressurised. The advantage initially was no one could tell if I was learning quick enough or indeed if I was any good, although that in short time could change. There was no smart ass breathing down my neck saying, 'What have you done that for, or you don't do it like that.' I was, if not my own boss, I was in charge of myself and certainly not pressurised.

Being the only one on maintenance and servicing it only needed very little knowledge to know more than anyone else. I had a list of customers and made my own rota for maintenance visits. There were emergency calls for breakdowns when again I was in charge. With the minimum knowledge I had gained I certainly knew more than any customer. But you sometimes met Brunel's incarnation who thought they knew the machine inside out. They would tell you what was wrong with it and what they thought was the cause of it. The temptation was to say well get on with it if you're so damned clever. The type of thing would be: 'The paper sometimes gets stuck, and I think it's the bottom roller that hasn't got enough pressure against the bottom drum or stencil. 'Well actually I think you'll find the driving cam when the machine is going to fast has a tendency to tighten the nut on the feed roller which restricts the through put of paper. The nut is known unofficially as the throttle nut due to its tightening, and you know what throttling does.'

Actually, half the time I hadn't got a flaming clue, but I knew more than the clever dick. The blinding of science is a wonderful thing or is it bullshit, whichever, it normally worked.

When Dennis had an appointment for a demonstration, he would ask me to get a machine ready to see if it was working OK. Only once did I fail. I either hadn't checked it or hadn't checked it thoroughly. The demonstration failed and he lost the sale. 'O dear, dear, not to worry.' Well do you think that was his reply, not exactly. He let me know his annoyance in no uncertain terms and rightly so, but that was the end of it, no recrimination. Within time I became proficient and indeed I am sure he was pleased if not proud of the service department.

Many of the locations where machines were installed were schools. One of these was a private school in the leafy suburbs of south Manchester for the sons of gentlefolk. Their duplicator was malfunctioning, so I was dispatched to repair the said malfunction. This machine was in an office next to the headmaster's. On completion of the repair, I knocked on the headmaster's door and entered on his command to inform him the repair had been completed. He had a slightly pompous air and the cut glass accent of an ex-colonel which he was, unfortunately this was delivered with a stutter. I do not wish to make amusement of anyone with such an affliction, but he delivered it with what you could call superior authority. Now a colonel with a stutter and quite a pronounced one is not what I would have thought conducive for such an occupation especially when giving an immediate order to fire.

On my return I was informed the MD wished to see me in his office. He informed me he had received a phone call from the said headmaster complaining I had burst into his office when he was in a meeting with his agent. I had been rude, arrogant and disrespectful, me never. I of course denied all such misconduct. Now whether subconsciously owing to his pompous air, I had expressed myself in the manner of his accusation, I was not aware. Obviously, this man craved deference, but Mr Britain the MD did not tear a strip off me, just giving me a slight censure .Living in the same leafy suburb as my accuser he may have met him or been aware of him. He did offer me some advice though, don't join the army.

I had been there now around six months and Dennis had taken a two-week holiday; an enquiry came in from a company who were looking for a new duplicator. Gordon Hyde the overall sales director for the company said he would cover the sales enquiries if I would assist him. We arrived at the company at the appointed time and were shown into the office where I set the machine up. A man arrived who was in charge of the purchase and introduced himself, Gordon who was a likeable and capable guy was not experienced with duplicators, his expertise lay in typewriters and calculators. His demonstration and sales pitch were hesitant and lacked the confidence and assurance which an experienced salesperson with this equipment would have.

If he couldn't answer a question, he would refer it to me. He didn't ask basic questions 'How often are you going to use it, what are you using it for, letters, posters, or more complicated items, how many people will use it, etc.," but he got through, but now it came to the most awkward part, removing the stencil. This actually was very easy, and you quickly got used to it, anybody not familiar with it could find it a little tricky. When selling a machine, it was important you made it look simple and easy.

The stencil is made of waxed paper, and measures 30x50cm, the wording to be reproduced is cut into it by placing it first into a typewriter. It is then positioned onto a nylon mesh screen on the duplicator which goes round twin cylinders, and the ink is forced through the screen and cut image in the stencil onto the printable paper. Before you remove it, you open a purpose made Manila folder to lay the stencil into. You then unclip the stencil with one hand and peel it away from the screen. Just as it finally unpeels you take a corner with thumb and finger, so then you are holding it top and bottom.

The side of the stencil that has been face on to the screen is full of ink, other than a 1cm border around the edge which is where you place your fingers. Once removed you quickly place it in the folder emphasising as little as possible the side with the ink and making it look simple. Gordon took the stencil off but did not get hold of the bottom and turned it round so the plain side was facing the customer, it was therefore hanging free. The stencils were very flimsy and could easily flap. The last thing you would want in this situation is air movement or a draft. And he got it. He was about 20cm away from the wall when the door opened. The stencil flapped and the corner caught and stuck onto the wall. He quickly removed it leaving a triangular patch of ink. We all stared in silence at this for a few seconds when Gordon responded, 'Don't worry it's water based go and get a rag out of the boot of my car.' I returned with the said item and he asked if there was a sink handy so he could wet it. The rest has gone down in the Reproduction department folk lore.

Water based it may have been, but it didn't say on the tin spreads like butter. This was a plain off-white wall which turned into one of the best abstract paintings you would ever wish to see. Gordon was a nice guy and had a good sense of humour and all credit to him he did see the funny side of it, all be it later. Don't mention this to anyone he instructed, especially Dennis. It would be impossible to keep it quiet especially as the room had to be redecorated. Dennis found it hilarious. Not that I ever told him of course.

My mode of transport since joining the company was a minivan which I could also use for domestic and pleasure I'm not sure where the domestic came in. The name of the company was emblazoned on the side with reprographic division, duplicators and copiers. I drove around 30,000 miles a year and did have two speeding tickets notched on my belt. The vast majority of the public's only contact with the police or brush with the law is via motoring offences, leaving murder, burglary, fraud and all other crimes to the minority. I was one of the vast majority living a blameless God-fearing life until I passed my driving test.

The rivalry between Manchester and Liverpool extends way beyond football it can manifest itself in many innocuous ways. The road connecting them is the East Lancashire Road this was opened in 1934 By King George VI and was the first purpose built intercity highway in the UK. It is a dual carriageway covering the thirty-three miles between the two cities. Depending where you live it only travels in one direction. If you are a Mancunian it only travels from Manchester to Liverpool, if you are a Liverpudlian it only travels from Liverpool to Manchester. One day when travelling some of these miles from Liverpool to Manchester on a derestricted section. I observed in the rear mirror a police car behind me. I continued for around a mile when it put on the siren overtook me and the stop sign came on. I duly obliged and wound down the window.

'Good afternoon sir,' said the officer, 'do you know what speed you were doing?'

'Around fifty,' I replied.

'Do you know what speed this vehicle is allowed to do?' he asked

'Well around the allowed speed limit,' said I.

'Yes, and the allowed speed limit for a commercial vehicle, is thirty miles an hour'

'But this is a minivan.'

'Yes, but it is classed as a commercial vehicle, and I'm afraid I am going to have to book you.'

'I had no idea of that,' I say. 'I know you have been following me for a good mile and I certainly wouldn't have been going so fast if I had known.'

So, book me he did. What type of police officer or indeed reasonable person, knowing the vehicle was the same size as a Mini and was well within the legal speed limit for that road, would do that? I would accept a warning could have been in order. But this guy had never read the police PR manual. And the police wonder why sometimes the public are alienated to them. To confirm the lack of commonsense, judgment or vindictiveness displayed by this officer, the law was changed shortly after, so small commercial vehicles were classified in the same category for speed regulations as a car. And that is common sense. Now there are certain times where happenings or circumstances are a life changing experience and this was potentially one of them. I had two speeding endorsements on my license a third and I could be banned. The consequence of that would be goodbye job. I would attended the case hearing, pleading Ignorance of the law, loss of job, ruined career, five children to support and any posterior licking mitigation I could think of. They had requested on the summons for my license to be sent to the court prior to the case. This was not obligatory, but I sent it.

The day arrived and at the appropriate time I was summand to the Dock. The three magistrates faced me on the bench and would you believe one of them was the boss of my Dad's company. You may wonder why this coincidence should be. The offence had occurred on the East Lancashire Road within the borough of Leigh and my Dad's company was in the Borough of Leigh. The said magistrate was a prominent member of the local hierarchy. I knew him, but from the brief and only time we had met, would he remember me, I think not. Would he realise I was winking at him or would he think it was an affliction in my right eye?

'How do you plead?'

'Guilty'

'You do realise Mr Williams that with a third endorsement you could lose your license?' the clerk of the court informed me, he continued 'Mr Williams has kindly sent his license into the court,' and with those few words I had the feeling he was on my side. I can remember the words clearly even today and how they were intonated especially the word kindly. My license was endorsed I was fined but I was not banned from driving. The affliction in my right eye was easily cured.

CHAPTER FIVE

The Next Step

Two years I had spent on the service side and I knew the machines backwards and in all other directions. It's time to start selling. The selling of this type of equipment was specialist selling. There are two types of selling, order taking or order getting. Order taking is selling the likes of beans or cigarettes they are marketed by the brand and by promotion and advertising and people know what brand they like. At the other end of the spectrum selling a jumbo jet is a little more difficult and certainly would be classed as order getting. Duplicators and copiers surprisingly could be classed in the same category but obviously way down the scale. The principle though for both is the same you have got to convince the buyer that this is the machine or aircraft for them. To make the job a little easier you have no need to convince them it is the finest in the world, but it is the best suited for their needs, after all very few people have a Rolls Royce.

The salesmen involved are professional, knowing the product they are selling thoroughly, and their competitors. They sell in a structured, ordered, planned and skilful way, and they are good at what they do. In the case of duplicators and copiers there is another element which jumbo jet salesmen would not encounter to the same extent. You have only one chance of selling it, you go to your appointment, demonstrate and hopefully sell the machine. The company will be also looking at two or possibly three of your competitors. Unless you have convinced the buyer that this is the machine for them you have lost, there is no going back. The old adage first impressions count is true, and if you are the first it is doubly true. You have to set the standard others have to better. You generally have no idea if you are the first or last, but you certainly know you will not be the only one.

You must know your competitors, their strength and their weaknesses, so you can counter with the advantage or benefit your product brings, but one thing you must not do is discredit them. Indeed, you should not mention them unless the customer does, to do so gives the indication you are very aware and perhaps concerned about them. Should the customer refer to one you could acknowledge it and say it is a good product. This implies you are not concerned about it, although you may be, you must not let the customer know. You must express clearly and implant in them the merits and advantages of your product. In the words of W S Gilbert. 'If you wish in the world to advance your merits you've got to enhance, you must stir it and stomp it and blow your own trumpet or trust me you haven't a chance.' I couldn't have put it better.

My boss Dennis was a very good salesman. He was the one who taught me to say only enough and get out. Concentrate on what needs to be said to obtain the sale. That did not mean you were abrupt or curt. Should the client talk about last night's football, holidays, or whatever, certainly engage with it, but do not expand it. Say just enough to complement it but do not be distracted from what you are there for. Salesmen do not have to be good talkers; they do have to be good listeners and receptive to the customers' needs and ones the customer may not even be aware of. The bad or dubious reputation that salesmen endure stems mainly from the fast talking here today gone tomorrow types who deal mainly with the public. The ones whose business is with the commercial or professional world cannot afford to deliberately miss sell or mislead. They are selling to either professional buyers or senior people who have on the whole reached their position through ability.

Well, that's good I've got that sorted, now I know exactly what to do, where's my first enquiry? I had done a few small sales for the low-priced copiers, but my main job was still maintenance and service. My opportunity came when Dennis handed in his notice. He had been a great boss and one I was very fond of, it had been a very friendly partnership rather than a boss and his assistant. I applied for the position but was not offered it, they were considering various options. I was now the only one in the Reprographic department. Until a decision was made on the appointment of a manager, I would service all sales leads and all maintenance and service enquiries. I would be provided with a big bass drum to put on my back, symbols to fix between my knees and a trombone. I could perform my sole position in the finest one-man band tradition.

On not being offered the position I was not overly disappointed or surprised I was only twenty-two, good heavens I was still young and carefree. All the academic and theoretical points I have previously mentioned on selling are completely irrelevant and superseded by the one I omitted, experience. The occasional selling I had done exerted no real pressure and it was usually of a small or second-hand machine to one person.

This was a world away from a £500 state of the art machine, with three people in attendance who needed convincing this was the one for them, come back Dennis. Luckily this situation was not the one I experienced with my first appointment. This was with one of the wet original type copiers and possibly a more sobering experience. These machines were very simple they measured approximately 40x30x25cm and were light in weight. They were simple having only a revolving light source a small motor and a developing tray. To produce a copy, you placed the original between two sheets of paper, one negative, and one positive. You then put the three pieces through the revolving light tube. Once through you took away the original and fed them through the developing tray, you then separated them and the image was on the positive paper, hopefully.

I had operated this type of copier dozens of times. I could operate them with my eyes closed so I thought. In my maintenance repair mode I would often wear an open neck shirt, not now, in my elevated sales mode, tie Savile Row suit, shoes shining enough to comb your hair in.

The circumstance that occurred was solely down to my sartorial elegance which obviously was not my natural attire. To place the papers through the light source you had to slightly lean over the machine, this I did with an obviously unjustified nonchalance. Suddenly there was a downward pull on my neck my tie was being developed along with the original around the light tube. This had obviously occurred because I didn't normally wear a tie when operating the machine it was probably enhanced by the distraction of talking and demonstrating. Whatever the reason, my tie was slowly going round the light, the immediate response is to pull upright which is not the thing to do. This would lift the copier and spill the developing fluid. My chin is now twenty centimetres above the machine.

The on/off switch which is on the front of the machine I am fully covering with the position of my body which is leaning virtually over the whole machine. I fumble with my hand in an awkward position to find it, while requesting in a calm, quiet, orderly fashion 'pull the plug out pull the plug out!' and someone kindly obliged removing the plug. My position was still twenty centimetres or now less above the machine and my tie was trapped, only one thing to do, take it off. Impossible with both pieces of the tie trapped. So, with the aid of a pair of scissors I stood in my Savile Row suit with a six-centimetre stub of tie. A prize will be offered to anyone who can find in any sales manual how to close a sale in such a situation, but thanks to the good humour and dash of sympathy expressed by the customer, combined with the excellent copies I proceeded to produce I closed the sale. Remembering my first ever call with the putty procurer I seemed to be making a habit of making an event with first calls but whatever the event I had got the order.

The company premises where directly in the centre of Manchester in a prime position on one of the main roads. This was ideal for promoting the company but owing to the parking meter restrictions not conducive for employees whose job necessitated coming and going throughout the day. My situation meant I may have to return two or three times in a day, this was between appointments and required changing machines and picking up and dropping off other equipment. There often was a very short time between appointments and if so, you were on the minutes finding or waiting for a meter which was not easy and was time consuming. You often therefore parked on double yellows or preferably in the back street behind the premises, which still had double yellows, but was not as obvious as the main streets. Another advantage, the back doors of our department opened directly onto it.

The parking wardens who patrolled the area were a microcosm of society. You got to know them, some to have a brief word with, others to have a much longer word with!! Some you would nod to, others maybe smile to, or maybe not smile to. There were ones who would have an appreciation of your situation and be a little tolerant, and indeed helpful. Others had appreciation but no tolerance and those with no appreciation at all. You could categorise them into three main types. The ones who had retired from the military, therefore used to discipline and order they often had a military bearing you could spot them a mile off, if they were on today be careful. The ones who had never held a job of responsibility or any form of power, and now they had it. They were the worst of the lot, and the decent fair and reasonable ones.

I had at one time perhaps five or six tickets which I used to leave along the dashboard for all to see, the company would not pay the fines, and people think a mortgage is a burden! The decent and fair ones would often knock on the back door and ask you to move the vehicle after perhaps giving you ten to fifteen minutes, fully acceptable they had a job to do just as I did. Others would give you nothing, one of the give you nothing boys was on this particular day. There was a knocking on the back doors, I opened them and there was one of our staff informing me I was getting a ticket, and the warden was there making it out. I immediately said I'm sorry I'll move it. 'I've made it out your too late' was the retort. The saying 'It's not what you do but the way that you do it' was never truer.

He could have said in a reasonable manner, 'I'm sorry I've made it out, and you know you shouldn't be parked here.' I would still have been annoyed but I believe I would have accepted his reply. But it was the offhand, aggressive, no consideration manner of his reply which tilted the scales, plus possibly the five tickets I already had on the dashboard. We finished up nose to nose with a millimetre between us, watched by a crowd who were passing or who owing to the raised voices had come out of the doors of our or adjacent buildings. We discussed the weather, flower arranging, holidays. Why he should threaten to see me in court with such convivial conversation I will never know! I took the ticket off the car screwed it up, threw it on the floor and told him to stick it up the appropriate orifice. We never did meet in court and indeed I can't recall seeing him again, I can't recall if I got another ticket or payment demand, I probably did. I would avoid paying the tickets for as long as possible and sometimes it paid off, if you'll excuse the pun. The occasional one got lost in the system and you never got a demand.

I have got distracted. My main occupation now was selling duplicators and copiers and to a lesser extent repairing them. I had made two sales since Dennis left and acquired one new tie always now tucked into my pants. The powers that be had appointed a new manager and he was due to start in one week. It was also decided to appoint someone to take over the repair and maintenance and I would be fully employed on sales, although I would still be required should the need arise to help with any repair and to give full training to the new recruit. The manager duly arrived, an ex-policeman with no experience of the reprographic industry but some in selling, the mind boggles. Who would employ someone to head a department with no experience of what they were in charge of? I presume the powers that be must have assessed he had potential or they wanted someone with influence who could reduce the number of parking tickets. He was in his mid-forties and seemed an ok guy.

I would now be training two people, this would certainly aid my authority, God if all else failed I could go into teaching. Jim Gaffney was his name and I quickly got to like him, which was a good start, he respected my position which was understandable considering his acquisition of knowledge was primarily dependent on me. I think there was a mutual respect. I imparted the knowledge with a fair attitude, withholding nothing, as against playing it close to my chest to retain an element of control. There was not the slightest element of I'm now the boss with him. Mind you he knew which side his bread was buttered.

He was a personable guy and I assessed once he mastered the machines, he probably would be ok. He certainly was different from Dennis who although married with two children had still liked his clubbing and female conquests. You would assess Dennis as a man about town, with a slight air of Jack the Lad about him, the archetypal specialty salesman. Jim was more a family man a nice guy, hopefully not too nice because this could be a hard game. He accompanied me on appointments and eventually started to take the occasional one his own.

Within two weeks of Jim starting the new service mechanic joined us, Matt he was around my age and a clever little sod, combined with an air that I didn't quite trust. A really likeable little shit. This I would play close to my chest; it was still in my interest to impart just enough knowledge but because he was such a know all he may not ask a certain question, and who was I to expand on it, if he's such a smart ass he could find out himself as I did. I hope that demonstrates the nice, helpful, caring side of my personality. So, we had a happy little band, well two-thirds of one.

I asked him one day to accompany me on an appointment, being in a considerate mood it would help him expand his knowledge forget that it needed two to carry the machine. This was at the site of the construction of the Rakewood Viaduct on the M62 and they required a copier on site, the demonstration was in the large site hut. At this time period there were three plug sockets in standard use. The thirteen-amp square pin, the Wylex with a large round centre pin and two smaller ones to each side, and the small five-amp three pin. It could be any one of these you found on arrival. You therefore left three bare wires on all machines inserting them into the socket and securing them with a plug from another appliance. The copier I was demonstrating had a timer which you set depending on what you were copying, and it was activated by pressing a button in the centre. The demonstration was going well producing good copies for all they required. The senior man of the two present suddenly commented abruptly, 'Why are the men leaving?'

On looking through the window there must have been ten men walking past the site cabin.

'It must be lunch,' volunteered the other

'But it's only 12.15,' said the senior. 'Has the siren gone?'

'About a minute ago' the other said

'Why?'

I then continued to make a copy and pressed the centre button the senior man said 'It's there again, it's when you pressed the centre button.'

'It can't be,' I said

'Try it again,' he responded

I did and sure enough the siren sounded. "Well, that's fifteen minutes lost time, times how many have left, off the price,' said number two jokingly (I hoped). The spare plug I had used was connected somehow to the siren electrics; I didn't investigate why. It was a rare occurrence and one I'm happy to say did not stop a successful sale, with no reduction for the hours of lost work. Another pleasant surprise, clever-dick did not try to tell me how it had happened.

What would you do how would you react if you could see your car being broken into, but you could do nothing about it? The CIS Tower in Manchester when completed in 1962 was the tallest building in the UK at 387 feet (ok, not as tall as Blackpool Tower but that's a structure not a building). I had an appointment and was waiting in reception on a floor up with the birds. There was one other man waiting and he was looking out of the window at the Manchester panorama, when suddenly he let out a shout, 'Hell someone is breaking into my car.' He could view his car in the street many feet below and observed a man opening the door and obviously helping himself to whatever treasures this driver had left. I went over to the window; the back door of the car was open, and I could just see the man's leg the rest of him was inside the car. The owner next to me was obviously agitated, he could not shout as the windows where none opening, obviously, so in case anyone wanted to prove Newton's theory was correct. By the time he had gone down the perpetrator would be well gone, so we just stood there and watched while he absconded. An unusual thing to witness and not to be able to respond and one that taught me never to leave anything on the back seat.

The department was working well. Jim was good to work with, Matt I worked with as needed but kept any sign of friendship to the minimum. There was no real pressure as

long as you performed. My sales were good we didn't have set targets as long as they were deemed satisfactory and made an overall profit. I won a prize for my sales performance a record player which we had for many years in fact things were really looking up. The minivan went, replaced by a Ford Escort Estate, a record player and new car is this the zenith of my career? I would service the enquiry if I took it over the phone or someone I had seen who came into the showroom. Jim would share other enquires between us, I probably had the greater. He would also have more paperwork and admin to attend to.

The writing down of the correct details of messages and enquiries is vitally important both in time and money. If it's a message or service enquiry and should it be mislaid they will probably phone you back not necessarily so if it's a sales enquiry. A young trainee service mechanic who was transferred from the typewriter department had joined us. He demonstrated the importance of this in his first couple of weeks. One such enquiry he took he gave to me; it was from a company called

Group Eleven Banks. There was a well-known company called Group Four Banks who transported money, but I'd never heard of the one who'd called. He had taken the address but not the telephone number and I couldn't find the number in the directory. Their address luckily was in an office block near to us, so I walked over. This was a seven-storey building. I trawled through most of the floors and offices asking if they knew of a Group Eleven Banks as I couldn't find them. I also asked if any had made an enquiry for a photocopier, one had, Gruber Levinson and Franks. Well, that's phonetics!

The majority of demonstrations and sales went without any real incident or problem with nothing particularly going awry, of course there were the exceptions as I have previously indicated. Although you were aware something could go wrong and you were slightly prepared for it, it was often the unexpected that caught you unprepared. On

selling a machine, you sometimes made a part exchange for their old one, this I had done with a duplicator taking in their old Roneo model. The Roneo was a different design to the one we sold, having a central cylinder into which you put the ink. The stencil then went onto the outside of the cylinder. When a customer wouldn't buy a new machine, you would offer them a trade in model so as not to lose the sale. Sometimes when it was not the make we sold they were checked, other times not. The customer with this particular enquiry only had a minimum usage so a low-priced second-hand machine was ideal. I had a basic idea of the Roneo model but had never operated one. I did a brief run through in the workshop to see it was working, and it was.

On arriving at the customer, I placed it on the necessary table and gave a brief run through to those in attendance. When selling a second hand or trade in machine you were never under the same pressure as selling a new one. You were really doing the customer a favour, providing a machine that would fulfil their needs and cost them the minimum. I was very relaxed and demonstrated how you put the ink into the inside of the cylinder through the filler cap. The ink then went through the fine mesh of the cylinder wall onto the stencil. The machine was an electric model. I pressed the switch to start and explained how the cylinder should rotate just a few revolutions to mix the ink before sending the paper through. The cylinder rotated when suddenly ink flew out of the filler cap hitting the ceiling and continued to produce a perfect line of blobs of ink approximately 30cm apart along the ceiling and onto the wall.

This had happened in the blink of an eye, your eyes were quickly drawn to it, but a few seconds elapse before realising what had occurred, recovering from shock and stopping the machine. As seems the custom in these situations you spend a few seconds along with the customer staring at the offending mishap. It's a combination of shock, disbelief, and how the hell am I going to get out of this. The first thing to do is apologise. Thoughts of Gordon and the stencil on the wall percolated my mind, but now I'm in charge. Learning from that experience I thought scraping it off may limit the spread, so I asked for a thin card and luckily one was quickly to hand. It did limit the spread but not the stain I reduced this with a damp cloth. After all it was water-based ink. It did unfortunately necessitate another repainting, at this rate we could start a decorating division. The cap was obviously strained through use. I wondered if I had looked at the ceiling of the company I had traded it in from, would I have noticed stains every 30cm. It's all experience my boy, you live and you don't learn.

Why is it that the remembrance of bad luck or misfortune seems perhaps more prevalent in the mind than good luck or good fortune? I would suggest that on the whole you have more of the latter, because the former is contrary to your desires, hopes, wishes it tends to be more memorable or noticeable when it occurs, it reduces progress and causes a blockage. Good luck and good fortune are what you should have and what you desire, therefore you accept them more as a right or norm, bad luck or misfortune, are often self-generated. Take the simple example above with the ink cap, you could say it was unfortunate that the incident happened, no it was my fault, I should have checked the machine thoroughly before I took it out.

Another example, I was going to a football match with a friend and he suggested we take a different route due to the traffic than the one I would normally take. So, I went with his suggestion and it cost me £60, I was caught in a radar trap for exceeding 30mph. Bad luck I should have gone my way, no I should not have been exceeding the speed limit. Don't look for excuses, fate and misfortune I accept in many instances you have no control over, you make decisions with the best will and logic, with an outcome of some you win and some you lose. I believe you should self-analyse and should you experience misfortune accept it, if underneath it is your fault. You know people who appear lucky, regularly winning on the premium bonds, racing, betting, slot machines, why they win is they spend, perhaps not as an addiction but enough to make it appear they are lucky, they never tell of their losses.

Over a lifetime luck and bad luck, fortune and misfortune, I believe on the whole average out. You have a very good job, but an unhappy marriage. You have a happy marriage but can't have children. You have a very happy healthy life enjoying all the pleasures of fitness. At forty you get a debilitating illness. Somebody with a debilitating condition from birth lives to cope with it and may not even think they are unlucky. There are a myriad of instances and conditions which you can attach fortune and misfortune to. But you are born with what you have got, and you have got to make the best of it.

Intelligence and certainly high intelligence, are a desired and respected commodity. But those who have it are born with it they have no choice whether they want it or not. I am sure most would want it, but perhaps don't realise their good fortune in having it. I met once a retired headmaster who had brought up a son with Down's syndrome. His wife had died when she was young. I asked if it had been hard bringing him up, 'No difference than any other child, 'was his reply, 'and there is one thing I have learned to have less respect for intelligence. 'What an interesting and telling thing to say from a man whose life was spent and dedicated to fostering and stimulating the thing we all desire. I presume he meant it was not the be all and end all we assume. His son had taught him other values.

You should work at and extend to their maximum the skills and attributes you possess for the benefit of yourself and humanity, and luck will be included in their development. Gary Player the great South African golfer offered a great observation, 'It's funny the more I practise the luckier I get.' And I'm sure it's true.

I digress, where was I? Oh yes selling, away with philosophising back to pragmatics. A new dawn was arising, the advent of the electrostatic copier. They eliminated the need for negative and positive papers you fed in your original and out came your copy. What are they you may ask? Allow me to enlighten you, electrostatic copiers use a technology called xerography. This is a dry process that uses electrostatic charges on a light sensitive photoreceptor to first attract and transfer negatively charged particles in a powder form onto paper in the form of an image. They were first brought out in 1959 and came into popular use throughout the 1960s. They were known in the UK as Rank Xerox produced in the USA by the Xerox Corporation and marketed in the UK by the Rank Organisation and they were the market leaders. Since then, others have come onto the market mainly the Japanese, Cannon being a prominent player. They were marketed at the medium to large volume user, so the existing wet process copiers were still required for the smaller volume users.

My company was a member along with other office equipment suppliers of an organisation based in London who supplied and manufactured products for the office market. They developed and brought out in the mid-1960s an electrostatic copier to be supplied through all their members. My company at last could compete with Rank Xerox, well not exactly. The negative charged particles in powder form as described in the

Xerox, were in this 'State of the Art catastrophe suspended in liquid, yes liquid, which had been the bugbear of the old type copiers. All be it the liquid was different, this was jet black and referred to as toner in the modern idiom and the problem was not just the liquid. It was the clanging banging of the chain driven movements, and the back of a cigarette packet design that produced its great appeal. The best description of this machine was provided by a children's TV programme shown in the 1950s. It was known as *Billy Bean and His Wonderful Machine*. It was introduced by a song, the words of which were as follows.

'Billy Bean built a machine to see what it would do. He made it out of sticks and stones nuts and bolts and glue. The motor sang chuffaty bang rattatarattatarator, and all of a sudden a picture appeared on the funny old cartoonerator.' If you don't believe me look it up. The guy who wrote this obviously had a premonition. It could not have been described better. It made anything described as 'Heath Robinson' appear like nanotechnology. And we were expected to sell it. We were introduced to it at an unveiling in London combined with a demonstration of its operation and world leading technology. The enthusiasm with which the sales team demonstrated and eulogised about its ground-breaking performance was in fact the most perfect demonstration of delusional enthusiasm you could witness.

All the other copiers or duplicators we sold were equal or in our unbiased judgment superior to our competitors, unfortunately Billy Bean's machine wasn't. We would just have to hope and pray plus any other external assistance that prospective customers did not also consider viewing the opposition. The only slight possible advantage in our favour was you could buy our machine, Xerox you could only rent, and that needed to be justified by the number of copies over a monthly period you required. The machine was also heavy, ideally it needed two on a demonstration that had an advantage in that you shared the lack of success. We sold a couple in the first couple of months we found the 90% discount helped.

An enquiry came in from a company in central Manchester housed in one of the old Victorian office blocks. I was the only one available to fulfil the appointment, and this contributed to what could have been the most expensive calamity, to add to the list of previous ones. The company was on the fourth floor. With the aid of the lift and my younger years I found the offices and readied the machine for the demonstration. The customer was of Middle Eastern origin, which often entailed their domiciled hobby of bartering or battering you down to a price they thought acceptable, and with this machine they held the upper hand.

I had concluded the demonstration successfully all that was left was the negotiation of the price he would pay. I will rephrase that omitting negotiation, he told me the price he would pay, which I did not accept. He then ranted on with why he would not pay more, how he prayed to Allah every day, and how his seven wives were very expensive. I countered by suggesting he joined the Methodist church then he could only have one wife. It actually deteriorated into a modicum just above a slanging match, I would not give ground, and neither would he. I was annoyed, he had offered me £10 for the machine and I wanted £15, not quite but the principles the same, and with that he stormed out of the room.

Now you may recall earlier I described how we left bare wires on the machine so as to accommodate whatever plug socket was installed. This as normal was secured by a spare plug, now this machine being the latest high tech one of its kind on the market had liquid which had to be pumped out of the toner tank by a tube into a container with the machine switched on. I had inserted the tube into the container, but the flow was intermittent, the pump kept stopping. I presumed therefore that the wires in the socket were not properly engaged making a bad contact. I went to the socket to address this. One of the wires was short so I tried to make a connection a number of times when I suddenly heard a shout. This was Middle Eastern Mans second-in-command. The tube from the tank had come out of the container and was lying on the large handwritten cash book (yes, they used to be handwritten) and the liquid was pumping all over it. I had never turned the machine off; I obviously had kept making a connection unknowingly. 'I'm going to get Mustafa,' he said, and I with the stout resolve similar to the cowards who run in my family, quickly decided I also Mustafa quick shuffty out of here. I grabbed the wires now secured by the plug and pulled them hard, stupid boy. This I had never done before. I think it was more in anger and frustration. They came away along with the socket from the wall and about a square meter of plaster, the socket dangling on a 30cm piece of wire, the plaster all over the floor Oh dear! Well, something like that. My anger and any other feeling turned to a low form of panic. I picked up the machine like a man possessed. Luckily, there was only the minimum of liquid left in it and scarpered.

I returned to the office anticipating being met by a delegation, who had assessed we now needed a building division in addition to the decorating one. Thus, ensued one of the biggest mysteries I have encountered even to this day, we never heard a thing, how, why, I cannot make sense of. The second-in-command who went to find the boss presumably never found him, I can only presume he's still looking for him. Well, that's solved that, and all this time worrying and wondering. I think it's time to move on before I bankrupt the company.

Where was I going what were the prospects, I had recently got married, a family may be near, I wanted broader horizons. A big game hunter would offer that, but very few vacancies around Manchester. This type of selling was quite a mercenary job in a way. You sold a machine and never saw the customer again, or very rarely. That is unless you had to redecorate their office or replaster their wall. I could keep a look out to join a manufacturer with more pay more prospects. I had spent five very enjoyable years which had furnished me with great experience, but with this Billy Bean Machine it was downhill from here. They say it's a poor workman that blames his tools, check that out with a Joiner who's got blunt chisels.

What makes a good salesman? One thing that stimulates your senses and keeps you on your toes is competition it can make you or break you. As US President Truman said, 'If you can't stand the heat get out of the kitchen.' With competition you have got to embrace it and enjoy it, it is part of the game. There is competition in many jobs and indeed in life, but it is not necessarily a specific or fundamental part, in selling it is. You're involved with competition to a more or less degree every day. Speciality selling as I've described, selling capital equipment is a very good training ground. You mainly have one chance to sell it, you therefore must be alert, receptive, productive, intuitive and enunciate all the benefits of your product, and you must enjoy it. Smile, it may not secure you the sale, but it certainly won't stop it. Know your product and the competition. Be positive in your answers and demeanour but never lie or pretend to know the answer when you don't, if you don't know say so. Be trustworthy this is fundamental, if you're not trusted you have no chance of success, trust if lost can never be regained.

Don't be smart or a Mr Know-all. Don't proclaim yours is the best product on the market, they'll never believe you (even though it may be) but it is the one best suited to their needs. Don't oversell, that is sell a product that will do more and cost more than they need, just to increase your turnover. You will lose out in the long run. And the most important of these is trust. I was once given confidential information by a customer who was a friend of my boss (nothing to do with him personally) he requested I told no one. Sometime later my boss found out and he was not pleased, but he knew I could keep a confidence. Considering I seem to know all the elements of how to make a success of selling, how come sometimes I lose out. Well obviously, somebody knows them better remember there's always a faster gun in the west.

CHAPTER SIX

The Beginning of the End

I scanned the paper most days, *Telegraph* of course, and within a short period one caught my attention. It was for a representative to cover the north of the UK for a French suspended ceiling tile manufacturer. Now that sounds different and interesting, as far as the product goes that would be a new start. I applied and didn't get the job, and then I did get the job. Work that one out, allow me, I received a letter thanking me for the interview and informing me I wasn't successful. Yes, the French have a myriad uses for their letters. I then received, a few days later, a phone call offering me the job. It had been offered to an ex-work colleague of the MD who after consideration had turned it down. His loss my gain, which it certainly eventually proved to be. I was in the same industry or line of business for thirty years until my retirement from my own company at the age of fifty-eight. That sounds very simple and straight forward so I'll finish here, but that would spoil a journey from the lows to the highs from desperation to success and all those imposters in between.

The year was 1971, I was twenty-eight married in a new house with a one-year-old son. The future looked bright and my enthusiasm reflected it. The company had offices in Surrey, and the MD who I was answerable to was based there, being answerable to the MD sounds good but so were the other four employees. This was not ICI. The head office in France was a different storey; this was based in the centre of Paris with a couple of factories in central France. The company was part owned by an American corporation.

My boss Ian, the MD, was a northern guy from Stockport. He had spent most of his working life in the industry and had been Northern sales manager for Armstrong Cork the world leaders in suspended ceilings. I seemed to specialise in joining companies or an industry as a rookie, but thankfully with very good and experienced bosses. I was to work from home using that as the northern office. There was a rep for the south east and one who was to join us some time later covering the Midlands. For my incubation period I spent a week at the head office familiarising myself with the products and being briefed on the industry and my job, this included two days going round with the south east rep introducing me to ceiling contractors.

Architects and ceiling contractors formed the principal focus for the sale and promotion of the product. The architects were the ones who would specify the product the ceiling contractors would then install – that is it simplistically. To a lesser extent developers, interior designers, main contractors and ceiling contractors could all have an influence on the final product used; you could never rest completely until the order was in your hand and the product installed. The week went well I got on with my colleague from the south and the MD. It was arranged that I spend a few weeks with a Manchester ceiling contractor on the tools and getting my hands dirty, it was a good learning experience. The time was spent on a number of contracts with different teams and varying types of ceilings. With reference to the learning experience there were two and I'm not sure which proved the greater. The knowledge acquired about the ceilings, or for the one and only time in my life being physically thrown out of a pub.

The last of the contracts was an office block on the edge of Moss Side the infamous Manchester suburb. The foreman was an Irishman called Billy (can I get away from them?). He was good fun and took me under his wing, he was helpful and informative. I decided at the end of the week to buy him a pint in appreciation of the tuition he had given me. Over the period from 12 to 2.30pm on the Friday he went missing, at around

2.35 his mate appears back on site. I tell him I was going to buy Billy a pint and he informs me he is still in the pub. Being new to the building trade I was naive to the traditions of the trade; Friday lunch is drinking time. 'It's only a couple of minutes down the back street,' he says. 'he'll be there.' Closing time was 3pm so off I pop. The pub was a true back street Moss Side boozer. You entered up three steps and through double swing doors. I went in and Billy was sat on the table immediately left of the door. What met me was a vision of black, Billy was dressed in black, the wrought iron table was black, and the top was a dark marble covered with Guinness bottles. 'I was going to ask you earlier if you fancied a drink,' I volunteered. 'Sit down I'll get them,' Billy replied and returned with a pint and two bottles of Guinness. 'I can't drink that it's ten to three,' said I. 'Get 'em down we've half an hour yet,' he said in a slightly slurred Irish brogue.

At five to three he got up and came back with two more bottles of Guinness. This was serious stuff, I had the pint Billy finished the rest, God knows what he'd had since 12.30. At around 3.20 after a couple of calls to drink up from the bar we duly obliged and went to the gents. There were two urinals, a man was stood at one Billy went to the other, I went in the cubicle. I could hear Billy muttering something and the man replying in a strong Irish accent, the conversation suddenly got heated and loud. I came out of the cubicle and they were facing each other with faces only six inches apart. The whole thing had flared up in thirty seconds, two Irishmen with Guinness coming out of their ears, sounds ideal for a prayer meeting. I was stood just watching them when the door burst open and the landlord entered with intent and a size to fulfil it. The man had his back to him. In a flash he grabbed his coat collar, moved slightly to the side and with his other hand grabbed Billy's collar. He swung the man around to face forward dispatching them through the door and marched them through the bar still holding their collars. I was following close behind. On reaching the doors he stopped and turned his head to look at me, before

I could react, his hand grabbed my collar raised me slightly, so I felt like a puppet moved behind me and pushed the three of us through the doors and down the steps. Billy and his co-defendant finished on the pavement; I retained my balance but not much else. From the landlord coming into the gents, it had taken no more than forty-five seconds to dispatch us onto the pavement. I helped Billy to his feet, 'Take me home,' he requested, I went for my car and granted his request. He told me on the journey he'd come over from Galway in Ireland as a young man as many of his generation did. His mother used to instil in him as a young man if ever he went to England be very careful where you go and what you do, always keep to the main roads never go down back streets. He said, 'I've been here thirty years and I'll tell ye, it's the bloody Irish you've got to watch not the English.' I never met Billy again, I found out a little later that his character and reputation proceeded him, well not a surprise, and I never did buy him that pint.

On reflection I did think the landlord's reaction was a little over the top, he could in a courteous respectful manner have asked us to leave, giving him the benefit of the doubt, he may have had a bad day and needed to vent his frustration, or he needed to practice his extraction of inebriated customer drill. Without a doubt he had certainly done this before and I presume experience prevailed, better to nip it in the bud than allow it to develop. As for me, I'm innocent your honour, but guilty by association, keep that in your experience of life log. It brought to mind my old mate Dave and his words as to why he had left a similar establishment, 'I was fed up with having no skin on my knuckles.' What a very memorable few weeks with one hell of a finisher.

The Monday of the following week was the first day proper on the job. My office until the phone extension was installed in the small bedroom was the hall table where the phone was, my chair was the second step of the stairs. I was sent every week a trade paper with new and revised listings of commercial building contracts throughout my area, this gave all the relevant information you needed to know, type of building, construction details, architect, developer, etc. You could then make the necessary appointments and chase the contract, with the intention of getting your product specified. This temporary office accommodation was not the easiest or most suitable to conduct business and this I soon discovered was compounded by my one-year-old son.

He would be happily playing in the lounge and then would decide to have a walk about he could reach the handle of the door and soon discovered how to open it. He would come down the hall as I was on the phone saying in his one-year-old talk 'Fine O Fine O,' this after a little pondering we realised was his translation of our phone number 51590. I would clasp my hand over the mouthpiece and wave my other hand directing him go back, while shouting for my wife to come and get him, simultaneously holding a conversation with a hopefully unsuspecting architect. It was the verbal equivalent of the trick of spinning plates on poles where the artist had to keep twenty of them going. Luckily this temporary accommodation soon metamorphosed into the luxury office accommodation of the back bedroom.

There were hundreds of contracts to choose from in the trade paper, you analysed and chose the ones you thought appropriate. The response from the architects fell into five categories; not in, not available, no interest, call back, call and see me. With their main attention focused on designing the building, the unlimited amount of phone calls they received from suppliers and manufacturers was a considerable distraction from their main focus. Timing was everything, you had to hit them ideally when they were about to consider your type of product, or when they had a little free time, these were the two main reasons for a positive response. Being a new product also gave me a slight advantage in arresting their interest. I made two or three appointments for the first week, considering the number of calls I had made, I hoped my success rate would improve with experience, but reality proved it didn't. You had to make a considerable number of calls for a minimal successful response.

Ceiling contractors were the other main focus for my attention they could have considerable influence on the product used. This could be exercised in a number of ways, they could put a product forward if none had been specified, they could change a specification or try to if they thought it would be beneficial them. They would do this mainly if another product was lower priced than the one specified it could be done at tender stage, submitting a tender on the one specified and putting an alternative forward with the lower priced one. Doing this could transfer some responsibility away from the architect to them should something go wrong. They may also promote a product if they thought it better or more suitable than the one specified. Some products or manufacturers they may not like or have had bad experience with, this also could have a bearing on their tender and response.

Once you had gained a specification you had to protect it until it was finally installed. This was done by calling on the ceiling contractors, confirming you had got the specification, and asking if they had received the enquiry and if they were tendering. If they hadn't received the enquiry this could work to your advantage, you could give them details of the contract and any main contractors you knew who were tendering. They could then chase the main contractors requesting to tender for the ceilings, should they then receive the tender enquiry or even go on to win the ceiling contract, this would ensure nothing would be changed with the specification. In addition, it would certainly cement a very good and hopefully lasting relationship with them.

When you had a specification for your product you could generally find out all or the majority of main contractors tendering, it was more difficult to find all the ceiling contractors who were tendering. Requesting information from the architects or surveyors was not always forthcoming, it could depend how well you knew them. You acquired more by calling on the ceiling contractors, gaining information and forming a contractual list. There was always a chance a ceiling contractor who you were not aware of or maybe you didn't know too well could get the job, this could be a slight concern if you were not aware of them had they changed anything.

Most ceiling contractors adhered to the specification there were the minority who you were slightly unsure of. The reps of some competitors also had a reputation of trying to change specifications to their product one in particular by coincidence was the one who originally was offered my job. He worked for another manufacturer and was a direct competitor. I was never aware he ever succeeded in changing one of mine. It was a cheap and backdoor way of obtaining business, and I don't think his reputation or standing with the contractors was very high. They would occasionally change a spec. if they thought it could be to their advantage, but they would do this through their own volition, not through being asked to do so. I never asked them to change a specification.

Should a contractor wish to put my product forward as an alternative to the one specified, I would offer my support and assistance, but the initiative had to come from them. Throughout my career I had great support from contractors obtaining many large contracts through their promotion of my products. It was a lead from one, which eventually enabled me to start my own business. They would only do this I'm sure if they had confidence and trust in me, I would never divulge information or details that were given in confidence, even if to do so would have been an advantage to me. To do so may be productive in the short term but certainly not in the longer one.

The first two months went very quickly, I was pleased with how it had gone, and I thought Ian my boss also seemed to be. I had to send a weekly report in so he could assess my progress. He decided to come up and spend a few days assessing my progress firsthand. Two weeks prior to this he had asked me to choose two architects who would be invited to Paris on a PR promotional exercise. I had met and made acquaintance with a number, but none as yet that I particularly knew well enough. One who had been very friendly when I had called to see him, held a senior position in one of the premier practices in Manchester. I thought he would be a good choice, so, I asked him, and he gladly accepted. On the day Ian came up he was looking through my reports when he came across the name of the one I had asked to Paris. 'I hope you've not asked this guy,' he said. The delay in my reply gave him the answer. 'Well yes I, I, have,' oh shit. 'Why'? I asked. 'Because he's the biggest sponger you could meet.' Well go to the top of the class in gullibility, and hand in your character assessment badge. 'Who else have you asked?' I gave him the name. Thankfully he didn't know it, which was fortunate because unbeknown to me, he turned out to be a friend or a close acquaintance of the sponger, well come on I was new at the job. Well after that embarrassment I enjoyed the few days with Ian, he was very well known to the contractors and many architects having spent most of his working life in the North.

I presume you know very quickly if you like or dislike a job, and I liked this job. I was travelling the whole of the UK from Cheshire, North. I was my own boss with a company new to the UK; it was up to me to develop the business with no prehistory, whatever was achieved was to my credit. As I previously mentioned taking an enquiry into a ceiling contractor was a very good way of cementing a relationship with them, this applied very much so to one of the large Manchester contractors. Chris the boss would corner reps if he saw you when you were visiting the company, by asking you in a meaning full Irish brogue, 'What enquiries have you brought us?' If your answer was none he would say, 'What are you wasting our time for then, we haven't got time to see reps, come back when you've got one.' You were best to answer in some humorous way, if you could think of one, having a sense of humour underneath his direct manner he would acknowledge an appropriate reply with a wry smile.

His company was installing our tiles on a job and I had arranged to meet him on site to go through the contract details.

A section of the tiles instead of going in a grid system were being fixed by adhesive direct onto the soffit. This was done by making five conical shaped dabs of adhesive about 2cm high onto the back of the tile. The adhesive was dark brown in colour with a heavy consistency and in no uncertain terms would stick to anything. Chris always wore a camel hair coat even when visiting site. We were watching a fixer putting the adhesive on a tile and in Chris's opinion and experience (he was originally a ceiling fixer) he wasn't doing it correctly. 'Give it to me, 'he says, the man hands him the tile which he then holds in his left hand. He takes the applicator for the adhesive which is like a scraper and from a tub puts five cones of adhesive onto the tile. He now has the tile in his left hand and the scraper in his right, with still a residue of adhesive on it. He walks to the ladder, stops for a moment and places the scraper under his left arm. He is now in front of the ladder with his back to us and the expletives start to pore, to the extent he would have made a sailor blush, he stays in that position for a few seconds probably too embarrassed to turn round. The fixer says in low tones to me, 'So that's how you do it. 'He then turns slowly round, with no let-up in the verbal dexterity. Our initial expression of suppressed amusement quickly became unsuppressed as he raised his arm and extracted the offending implement from its unintended housing. It was one of those absentminded moments you can't explain or indeed forget. Whether the camel hair coat he continued to wear was the same one or new I never asked

One of the necessities and sometime pleasures of this job was driving thousands of miles a year. The benefits included the freedom it gave, seeing the country, visiting new areas. The possible consequence of such extensive travels was now ten seconds before me, namely death. I was travelling north on the M6, my first awareness of my impending demise was earth being thrown in all directions perhaps half a mile ahead. A lorry was coming across the central reservation with a trajectory diagonally across the three carriageways I was on. The accepted advice in an emergency is stay calm, I wonder who thought that one up. I was in the middle lane a car was in the slow lane to my left level with me, I slowed as he did. Do I stop and be like a sitting duck and trust the lorry keeps the same trajectory and goes across to the front of me? If he heads straight for me, do I swerve to the right onto the central reservation? I couldn't go left, the car in the slow lane was stopping me, I could do with a bit of time to think about this. The lorry turned onto the fast lane, as it drew near, I could see the white of the driver eyes while he seemed to be fighting with the steering wheel, he passed me a metre away. I looked at the driver in the car to my left he looked at me and drew his hand across his forehead with a raising of his eyes. I looked in the mirror the lorry had stopped on the central reservation. Well just part of the hazards of the job, and very good fortune. Shortly after this near crash barriers were installed on motorways with my full backing.

After two years I had established myself reasonably well within my appointed area, Ian announced we were to have a sales competition. There were three reps covering three areas, the North the Midlands and the South, all three of us got on well, there was no overt rivalry. We were on a straight salary with no commission but there would be a prize, a picnic hamper. A what? Well, it would have boiled ham and goodies in it. The only prize worth winning therefore was pride, not that I went out every day with a determination and burning ambition to win, but it heightened your resolve. I had a very good relationship with ceiling contractors, and this proved a winning formula at the end. The ceiling contractor who had won one of the largest ceiling contracts in the North had put our product forward and we got the order. This is how as I had mentioned previously a contractor can influence a contract, and I won the Hamper 'Yippee.' It was like winning a food parcel, why can't they pay me more then I can afford to eat. The pride and satisfaction tasted much better than the boiled ham. Things were going well with my newfound status as a top rep, well for the time being, never delude yourself I may be bottom of the pile next year.

The competition must have increased our sales the three of us were invited to Paris, obviously to show the French how it's done. That is, how to appear business-like, efficient, articulate (well, in English) all with a blinding hangover. On arrival we were shown around the head office, for God sake let's get this over quick and hit the town, and hit the town we did with the guidance and generosity of our French hosts. At around 11.30 they offered to run us back to our hotel. They reminded us tomorrow was a busy day. We were being picked up at 8.30 and driven for four hours to one of the factories. We thanked them but we would enjoy the walk back and soak up the ambiance of night-time Paris. 'It's quite away they informed us.' 'Don't worry we'll be fine.' Four and a half hours later on finding the hotel (they had moved it three times in the night) we were not what could be described as fine.

The trouble with Paris is, one, the wine, the other is in the centre of many boulevard junctions there is statue of some long dead Frenchman set in a commanding pose pointing up one of them. This may be acknowledging some noted French military victory, well perhaps not (I'm not intending selling this book in France.) or may be a far-off colony. Unfortunately, we concluded due to copious amounts of wine and a little fatigue, he was with typical French Entente Cordial kindly directing us to our hotel. To this day, we are still convinced it was a deliberate French ploy played on the Brit's to send them anywhere but where they wanted, bed fully clothed, well it would save time in the morning.

Being a Northern lad when we were out eating, I received the usual ribald comments when presented with a gastronomic French menu, 'He only eats tripe, 'which is not true, I also occasionally eat other things. On the journey south we stopped for lunch at a very typically French chateau. I was still feeling the after effects of the previous night and the journey hadn't improved them. One thing I can eat when feeling queasy is tripe. It is in a way bland and slides down. And so, to the amusement of all present I asked if they did tripe. And to my and everyone's surprise, 'Certainly, sir,' said of course in a French accent. Now why you may ask did I think being in the middle of France it would come as a piece of plain honeycomb like I bought on Bolton Market. Perhaps it's because being typical English abroad, that's how the way we do it well the French don't. This came in a stew with god knows what else. About as far removed from the bland easy to slide down gourmet dish I was anticipating, I didn't ask for seconds, but it did stop the 'He only eats tripe' comments.

The trip south to the factory was interesting, informative and a little eventful. Throughout the tour and subsequent meeting little hints were dropped of how well the German operation was doing and they certainly seemed the flavour of the month. Whether this was true or a deliberate ploy to get us fired up we'll never knew. On the return journey our host who was driving commented how low he was getting on petrol. He informed us he was not turning off the Motorway, as to get back on he would have to pay another toll. He would try and make it to the next service station, he didn't, and the Three Stooges pushed the car to it. We made the suggestion that the Germans wouldn't have been so generous or willing, no more mention was made of them. Sometime later it was revealed why they had appeared so successful; their warehouse was stuffed full of stock and very little sold. Germany 0 England 1.

The five years I spent with this company were enjoyable and rewarding, forming the foundation for the rest of my working life. It opened up a new world from the more parochial one I had known. Travelling the country and abroad, being in charge of my own area and destiny, what effort I put in and success I achieved would be my reward.

Things were happening to the company in France, there was rumour of a takeover or merger which was bringing some disquiet to myself and colleagues about the future of the British operation. I now had five years' experience in this industry and had acquired the superior or toffee-nosed air of a ceiling rep, developed through spending most of your day looking up at a ceiling. This was in contrast to the flooring rep, who developed an air of inferiority and defeatism through spending most of his day looking down at the floor. I decided it was best to seek pastures new.

Although I left in 1976, I still have a connection to this day with the time I was with this company. When I first joined, I was down at the head office in Surrey for one of my periodic meetings when Ian my boss asked me 'You live in Bolton, are you near Edgworth?'

'Yes' was my reply.

'That's handy,' he says. 'My brother lives there, could you drop off our Christmas presents for me?'

And so, I obliged. We moved to Edgworth a couple of years later and became great friends, and still are with Joan his sister-in-law; Keith his brother died some years ago.

CHAPTER SEVEN

A Different Tack

I applied for a rep's job with a manufacturer of metal ceilings and claddings, the ones I had cut my teeth on were mineral fibre. I was of course familiar with the metal type having been in competition with them in my burgeoning career. It was not a matter if you can't beat 'em, join ' em, it was more to do with the spice of life variety, combined with that un-buyable commodity, experience. They were used mainly in a different type of building contract. The company was small compared with the one I was with. They were based in the Midlands and manufactured the ceiling and cladding system under license from a Dutch Company in Rotterdam. There were two other licensees, one in the South and one in Northern Ireland. This made for an interesting or possibly worrying combination, three companies all selling the same product throughout the UK. This offered another dimension to the situation of contractors switching specifications. You could obtain a specification and the contractor could give the order to one of three companies. In addition, they could switch it to a similar system supplied by the largest manufacturer and market leader. How the hell do you keep tabs on that lot, sounds ideal for a masochist or insomniac. There was no car supplied with this job just a whip and sleeping pills, and I'd applied. What the hell, are you a Man or a Mouse? The worrying thing I liked cheese. 'Well, we'd like to offer you the job Mr Williams' (was I the only one who'd applied?).I'll take it, and there's confirmation I was a closeted masochist and I never knew. Remember lad head up, keep looking at the ceiling never the floor and eventually it proved a wise decision.

In my three previous jobs I had enjoyed a very good relationship with all my bosses enjoying a friendship as well as a working relationship. My new company was no exception. They were a young company and the age of the directors matched this. My direct boss one of the three directors was probably only three years older than me.

In an occupation where you work closely with your superior it is vitally important you both like each other and have mutual respect. I cannot see how you could make a success of any career and certainly in sales if this did not apply. We had great fun and the atmosphere and ethos was one of enjoyment. This of course could only apply if you were doing your job and bringing in the sales. I can assure you there would be no fun no humour and no enjoyment, if at the end of the month you had a blank sales sheet. Luckily this did not apply. Luck though by itself was not sufficient but with hard work, determination, and enterprise, the luckier I got.

To demonstrate the fun and easy-going nature of the company (I emphasise again as long as you produced the goods), I met my boss Ken in Glasgow and we had a week calling on the ceiling contractors and architects in Glasgow and Edinburgh. We decided to make a call on one contractor who was a few miles out of the city and who I had only infrequently called on before, and after this encounter I would never call on again. We introduced ourselves at reception and asked to see Mr Fraser whom I had never met. Mr Fraser took his time maybe five to ten minutes. How do you fill this time void, by having fun of course, with the attractive receptionist? Ken affable, sociable, fun loving, fuels the humour, and then Mr Fraser arrives with a face that would have made Norah Batty look ecstatic. I then realised I may have got it wrong; his Christian name was Fraser and his surname Dour, Fraser Dour.

Now whether Mr Dour deliberately took his time to emphasise his authority or indeed was engaged in other matters will never be known. But one thing is certain, for part of the time he was deliberately listening to the frivolous innocent frivolity emanating from reception, and he obviously could not stand laughter. His enjoyment was the highland fling in hair underpants. I was just about to introduce us when he interrupted me with the never to be forgotten words, 'I believe you're drunk!' Now I have to say I was not expecting that especially as we were stone cold sober, I swear it your honour. Could he not tell for God sake when a man was drunk? What was even more surprising this was coming from a Glaswegian. He'd obviously never embraced the city's reputation. I'll wager a Saturday night in Glasgow had never belonged to him. I recall for a few seconds we were taken aback and then with the total surprise and the absurdity of the situation we started to smile was this for real? My retort if I recall was of the nature, 'Mr Fraser we certainly are not drunk, and if you can't distinguish between a man who is stone cold sober and one who is drunk you have a problem,' and with that we left.

On getting back to the car we were amazed and amused at the unique occurrence, embracing the funny side of it. 'Is this the last call?' asks Ken. 'Yes' 'Well let's go for a drink.' I'm afraid I never touch the stuff, before five o-clock'; but laughing boy did have the last say. On phoning the office Ken was informed a Mr Fraser had been on the phone complaining two representatives had called on his company and they appeared drunk. If he'd only known one was the boss, he could have saved a phone call. Let's hope they never have an order to place.

With two other companies selling the same product and a very active market leader there was no time for complacency, but I held my own with some to spare. When you obtained a specification, you had to be tenacious in tracking and controlling it. The specification would mention the name of the product but very infrequently the licensee. You had to ensure therefore all contractors tendering knew it was your specification and not one of the other two licensees. It was not easy to find all those tendering, there may be four or five main contractors tendering for the main contract. They would each send an enquiry out to a number of ceiling contractors and you had to try and find these during the tender stage. You could always find, at the end, which main contractor had won the contract and therefore which ceiling contractor they had appointed. The successful one may have had discussions, assistance and prices (which in theory but not necessarily in practice should all be the same) with one of the other licensees during the tender stage and their allegiance would be with them.

The two market leaders one who produced metal ceilings similar to ours, and the other who produced the more common mineral fibre type, both held what would be called promotional bashes. These were quite formal suited affairs held in a hotel with a sit down meal and a guest speaker, possibly a sporting or well-known personality. The invited guests were ceiling contractors and architects hopefully seduced into using their products. My company did no such promotional event, nor did the other two licensees. Right let's do something about that thinks I, and my company as ever were up for a good bash.

On a local canal there was a large canal boat that ferried day trippers up the cut, to wonder and gaze at the beautiful flora and fauna. I had heard it also travelled at night were the occupants also gazed in wonder but not at the flora and fauna. The guest personalities performed in their finest birthday suits exhibiting their artistry along the narrow gangway running down the centre of the craft. Would the invited guests who were only used to the more formal gatherings enjoy this, is the Pope a Catholic? And enjoy it they did as the demand for the second year proved. In the following months it lubricated the locks of normally restricted office inner sanctums, and meeting those who never came but who certainly wanted to the next time. It was the best £1000 on a promotion we could ever wish to spend and was paid for many times over. Its success even reached one of the market leaders in London. I met one of their management sometime after the event. He commented he wished they could do a similar one, but it would not be conducive with the image of the company. And there is a lesson to be learned. If you enjoy a good time, don't create an image.

After eighteen months in the job the Dutch company invited the reps from the three licensees to Holland. The group also included representatives from licensees in Europe and one from the USA. We were given the usual pep talks and factory tour, and the opportunity to meet and access our fellow incumbents. With the official business and indoctrination concluded, our hosts invited us to hit town. Now this is where I thought I'd impress, not probably having done so during day. They were starting in a few bars and finishing up with a meal. Well, says I 'If you will excuse me, I'll miss the bars and catch up with you for the meal. I am going to go to the Rijksmuseum to see the great Dutch masters, being here is an opportunity I don't want to miss.' Their immediate reaction was they wanted to check my temperature. Their shock and mine was even more compounded when Ronny Carter the Scottish rep for one of the other licensees said he'd come with me. So off we trot. My love and appreciation for art I got from my father, it came from all the paintings he brought home which he'd won on the fair.

The Rijksmuseum houses all the Dutch masters including *The Night Watch* by Rembrandt, this measures 363x437cm (12'x14'6"). It is not just the great size of the painting which is exceptional., it is also the use of light and shade which Rembrandt was a master of. This combined with the detail of all the characters and overall composition makes a truly magnificent work of art. We made our way through the gallery stopping and eulogising over the genius our eyes beheld. On stopping at one such master I could not make out the surface of the painting. It appeared to be glass which would be most unusual, therefore, to satisfy my curiosity I leaned across the protective rope barrier. Using the knuckle of my forefinger very gently I touched the surface of the painting with an equal pressure of a fly's footfall, obviously an overweight fly. The responding cacophony of sound from the alarm was intended to bring Amsterdam to a halt. Stick to your ground lad, Ron thought differently. I turned my head observing him making a fast arrow like trajectory to the far corner door. Now the Dutch are the tallest race in the world, unfortunately Ron was not blessed with Dutch extraction. Appearing swiftly around the door as Ron reached it and nearly colliding with him, was an attendant who personified the acclaim given to his fellow men. He looked into and around the room with an intensity and urgency that appeared not to have noticed Ron. Considering they were only 6" apart, this lack of apparent observation was in no short measure due to the 12" difference in height. The only shock he had was finding Ron under his chin. I stayed looking at the painting he came into the room looked around and walked out, without saying a word.

We concluded our memorable tour, hailed a taxi and met the others in the restaurant. We inflicted on them our cultural experience and advice on how not to steal a painting from the Rijksmuseum. We were due to fly home the next day. I was flying to London, Ron was flying to Glasgow. The others were staying another day. My flight was delayed for an hour and while waiting I engaged in conversation with the man sat next to me. He readily revealed he was British and lived in Geneva and was the European accountant for an American oil company. He had been sent by the company president to investigate and try to bring to justice the manager of their Rotterdam operation, who had absconded with a one million dollars and 35cents, obviously putting his hand in the till before he left. He had informed the president there was nothing they could do, and they would have to accept the loss. Very strange considering the amount involved. On boarding the plane, we sat together as the seats were not pre-booked. The period was the late seventies. There was at this time a well-publicised problem with the numerous crashing of the Lockheed Starfighter. The problem seemed to rest with the unfortunate pilots not so much with Lockheed which seemed to have no problem in selling them. I was sat next to the window and observed some distance away a military jet. This was not necessarily a Starfighter as I wouldn't have known one if I was sat in one. I commented on how unusual it was to see a military jet at an airport and alluded to the well documented problems of the Starfighter and how strange that governments were still buying them. This ignited from my new found friend the out poring of, in retrospect, repressed confidential information the like of which I have never experience before or since.

Previous to his current position he had been the European finance director for the Lockheed Corporation. He had been asked to leave due to the imminent arrival of a US senate committee who were coming to investigate the finances of Lockheed in Europe. He openly explained Lockheed thought it better if he was out of the way, and I'm sure that enabled him to buy a few cups of coffee. He then continued from Rotterdam to London to explain the liberal accounting practices in which they engaged. They had bribed politicians and senior military officials in Germany, Japan, Saudi Arabia, Italy, Greece and the Netherlands, to name but a few. They had paid the Greek colonels millions before they were ousted. Prince Bernhard husband to Queen Juliana of the Netherlands was paid one million to influence the Dutch government in their decision. He never dropped below a million whoever he mentioned. There was an Arab in London who was Mr Fixit or the go between. The conversation was jaw dropping especially for a Northern Lad whose payment in bribes was tripe and black puddings.

The Lockheed scandal broke to the world later in the year and revealed and confirmed a lot if not all of what I had been told. I followed it closely including an interview on TV with Mr Fixit in London. The fallout was extensive and worldwide. There were prosecutions, resignations, careers and lives' ruined. In Japan an actor Mitsuyasu Maeno flew a light aircraft into the home of Yoshio Kodama the underworld figure and Mr fixit in Japan as a protest to his involvement. Maeno was killed Kodama was uninjured. The chairman, vice chairman and president of Lockheed all resigned. The payments amounted to hundreds of millions. It played heavily in the formation of the

Foreign Corrupt Practices Act which president Jimmy Carter signed into law Dec19th, 1977.

Why the ex-finance director chose to reveal all too little me six months before it became public, I don't know, he operated in an alien world far away from my two meat and two veg domain. Perhaps it was a form of release to a stranger who posed no threat. I was an eager listener and he had nothing to lose, and for a brief moment he provided a window on the inside world of global business. We landed at Heathrow shook hands, and wished each other well, he off to his two up two down cottage in Geneva and me to my three up two down semidetached in Bolton. Now back to this planet, where I am tomorrow? Ah yes Barnsley. I need to get those samples ready.

With my feet on the ground but my head still in the clouds I took up the cudgels of my career. My company installed the cladding products in addition to manufacturing them. This on the whole proved an advantage. One other licensee also installed but their market was mainly down south which didn't impact on me, the other one only manufactured. Offering both services increased the value of the contract which aided my sales figures, it also alleviated the necessity to court the cladding contractors, being in competition with them did not endear you to them. This of course was completely contrary to the ceiling products where we needed the ceiling contractors to install them. Installing the cladding did though have a slight detrimental knock-on effect with the ceiling contractors. The rumour circulated that we as a company also installed ceilings. This was probably originated and certainly fuelled by the competition. Ceiling contractors would not be keen to price or install a product that was also installed by the product manufacturer, and they certainly would not promote it, I had to convince them this was not the case. The majority accepted it, but it was an unwelcome addition to the many elements involved in the promotion of a product.

The ability to offer a complete package for the cladding offset any occasional misunderstanding arising with the ceilings. There was the odd ceiling contractor who would raise the subject but in time it receded causing no major problem.

I had never understood why the Dutch company marketed and manufactured their ceiling and cladding products through licensees. They manufactured window blinds and sun louvers themselves in the UK and were fully capable of producing the products we made. At last they saw the light, if they'd only spoken to me in the first place; they decided to manufacturer themselves. This meant my company would just install the cladding. The four reps from the licensees were invited to join the Dutch company. Before I left I was chatting to the MD about the move and he thanked me for my contribution over the four years and wished me well, and a tip when you move he said increase your expenses. I wonder why he never offered me that tip three years ago. And all this time I was under the impression it was my sales record that had saved the company.

I and the other Northern rep split the country from the midlands to the Scottish border, me to the west him to the east. The Scottish rep, my fellow art lover Ron, kept Scotland, and the southern rep kept the south east. What a happy merry little band. How this would work out what it would be like to work for them was unknown. I knew the sales director who was my direct boss having met him at sales meetings and social occasions and he seemed a good guy, I was confident I could work with him. It was a new setup exciting in a way but slightly wary in another.

The company decided to have a stand and exhibit at the National Building Exhibition in Birmingham. The four reps manned the stand over the week which was populated with visitors from around the world. You met an interesting and varied clientele. One such person I spoke to was from Nigeria. He looked at various products one of which was a cladding product called 'Sandwich Wall,' it was made with a foam core sandwiched between two outer layers of aluminium. He picked up a small sample and asked, 'Can you eat it?' 'Are you speaking of yourself or lions?' I enquired he didn't reply, just shrugged his shoulders and walked off. This encounter may necessitate another string to my bow an improvement in my culinary skills.

The new operation had been working for about a month when I received a phone call from my old boss with the French company. He explained, a large engineering company in the Midlands were looking to produce a metal suspended ceiling system similar to the one I sold with my present company. He had suggested my name to them as a possible candidate to lead the sales and marketing of the new product. Was I interested? Just tell me when I can start! He would get them to ring me and I would take it from there, and ring me they did.

CHAPTER EIGHT

The End of the Beginning

The company was privately owned and one of the largest section rollers in the UK. Section rollers are companies who form metal into linear formed sections like railings or the sliding runners in a filing cabinet and the thousands of other products in everyday use. The forming of linear strip aluminium ceiling panels was ideal for them. What they manufactured was mainly always a component of a final product produced and marketed by someone else. They did not produce a named or marketable product of their own. The ceiling system would be the first time they had done this and therefore a completely new venture. They were a large company. I was interviewed by the MD and founder, he was a down to earth, no nonsense Brummie engineer who had started the company in the back room of his house, forming the lengths of metal through the removal of his back window into his yard. I liked him and the feeling must have been mutual because I got the job.

I was based at home and my area was from the North Midlands to the tip of Scotland. My ex-boss who had introduced me to the company had his own ceiling supply company and he had the agency for the south east. I was involved with the production of the new literature and advising how the ceiling industry works. My job was not sat in an office as a marketing executive but on the front line to get orders, and in retrospect I was naïve. There was no real money thrown at a marketing budget; I had new literature, the industry magazine, listing all new contracts and a briefcase. My competitors were well established ceiling companies with considerable marketing budgets and numerous reps on the road.

The literature took some time being produced in the meantime I called on ceiling contractors and informed them of my new company and product. The company was known by a few, the ceiling product unknown by anyone. Once the literature was available, I started following up the contracts with architects. It was a slow grinding process. From an architect specifying a product to installation on the contract could be from nine to eighteen months or longer. Ceiling contractors, as I've previously mentioned, could lessen this time by putting your product in a contract they had, as an alternative to the one specified, but this would be very unlikely with a new untested product. In addition, this type of metal ceiling was not as prevalent in everyday type contracts as the generally used mineral fibre products therefore there was less opportunity to substitute them.

The harmonious relationship I had enjoyed with all my colleagues in my previous employment was being strained in my new employment. This was only with one person. He was younger than me and on the sales of certain steel sections sold to ceiling and roofing contractors. He had been partly instrumental in the decision by the company to produce a metal ceiling. I had to work quite closely with him and could get on with him in certain respects. I respected his enthusiasm and ability. He was helpful and often assisted me whenever I required. He was though, very ambitious and I was very wary of this. It came to a head when he told me I answered to him, and I told him I do not, I answer to the MD. This he did not like, he said he would speak to him which I'm sure he did. No more was heard about it and it was never mentioned again. Our relationship after was fine although I always held a slight reserve.

It was an unusual situation, I did not have a direct boss, I did report to and see the MD every month, but he was not involved with my operation on a day-to-day basis, like a sales manager would be. They had people over sales in the various divisions, but none involved with me. I did reports on the contracts I was working on and the few specifications I had acquired, these of course were long term. The thing that was lacking was orders, eureka, I got one.

A friend of mine was opening a shop and required a suspended ceiling. A small job but you've got to start somewhere, I arranged for two ceiling fixers John Novak and Graham Good to install it. They were finding it difficult owing to their unfamiliarity with the system and odd shape of the shop, so I asked a third one Andy Still to assist them and use his expertise and with that they were Still Novak and Good. So, I asked the shop fitter if he would install it, I was up and running, well, the ceiling was. Two days later my friend rang me. 'Is this ceiling meant to rattle when you walk on the floor above?' he asks. 'You've got the rattling type for the same price as the non-rattler.' Now in all the buildings in all the world, the very first job had to be in a building with a wooden floor. The vibration when it was walked on caused the ceiling suspended from it to rattle. If this had been suspended from a concrete floor which was the conventional structure where suspended ceiling where mainly installed, there would have been no vibration and no rattle, simple remedy, change the floor to concrete. Next job please.

The cause of the problem was the rounded sides of the panels were not tight enough when clipped onto the carrier, producing a slight movement. I spent a day squeezing the panels with my hand to solve the problem. Thank goodness it was a small job. It was a lesson and luckily one that was not costly to remedy. With all the in house testing that can be done, there is nothing that equals an actual contract in the marketplace for finding faults and flaws. The problem was overcome by bringing the sides of the panel slightly inwards. Although not large it proved a useful contract. Now where is my second order coming from?

The lack of orders was a concern more to my company than to myself I knew eventually they would come. I had now obtained a few specifications, the orders for which would not be forthcoming for some considerable time owing to the reason I previously explained. To wait possibly twelve to eighteen months for an order was an anomaly to them. Normality was receiving an order and delivering it in one or two weeks. The company had my reports and were aware of all of these specifications. They applied no overt pressure but I was aware of their slight impatience and lack of appreciation of the situation.

Metal ceilings offer a number of advantages over the mineral fibre systems, but one they don't possess, unlike the mineral type, is the capability to absorb sound, in many installations this is important. The ceiling is the main surface area to absorb sound and offer acoustic correction, to compensate for this acoustic insulation is placed on the back of the metal ceilings. The ceiling panels have small perforations or a gap between each panel, the sound passes through these and is absorbed by the insulation. These are made mainly of low-density mineral or glass fibre wrapped in various coverings and supplied in tile form (called pads) or rolls. I was instrumental in finding a manufacturer and product we could offer along with the ceiling.

The main manufacturer of these pads, in fact the only one, was a company in the Midlands whose main operation was the manufacture of insulation for power stations and other large users. They had a separate division for making the insulation for the ceiling products. Although this was a smaller operation than their main activity it had by far the monopoly throughout the country for these ceiling materials, and their prices reflected it. I had a meeting with them and got all the information required to supply the products whenever we got the elusive order. Through my investigations I found another company in the northwest a specialist insulation converter who, although they had never made the type of product we required could easily do so. What was more important their prices were much lower. This find was to prove even more crucial in the not-too-distant future.

I had enjoyed a good relationship with most ceiling contractors throughout my career. I had received from them leads to chase, promotion of my products on contracts, and one such lead was now to prove vital and life changing. I called on this particular contractor, whom I knew well, every couple of months. We shared the same sense of humour and spent more time in humorous banter and jokes, amazingly he mentioned business. He had received an enquiry from British Nuclear Fuels. They were looking for a suspended ceiling to go in a reprocessing plant. There was no product specified, but a metal type would be the most suitable, and he gave me the contacts. I've had a couple of situation-changing events in my career which you could say had an element of luck. Calling on chance as I did, he could have been out and I would not have called for another four to six weeks, by then he may have forgotten about the job or most likely it would have been specified to a manufacturer, and the rest of my life therefore would have been different. I contacted BNF and made an appointment for a site visit.

The visit went well; we discussed their requirements. It would require a ceiling panel made specifically for the job, and the area being over 3000m^2 would justify this. They requested a small mock-up ceiling to trial and test. I had a meeting with our technical director who confirmed we could produce the panel. I needed samples to install the mock-up and I needed them quickly. I was reasonably confident we were the only ones at the moment involved, it was therefore important we kept our prime position. After a week I still hadn't heard anything about the samples but received a phone call from the head office, could I come down for a meeting with the company finance director, and at the meeting he dropped the bombshell; I wasn't being given samples but three months' notice.

They had decided owing to the increasing cost with as yet no return, to pull the plug and call it a day on the new venture. The cost incurred being my salary, my car, my working expenses, oh yes and the literature. If they thought they would get instant success on that budget they were short-sighted. I referred previously to how easy and obvious it was to assess the success of a rep, due to his sales or lack of them, well say no more. Although it was a shock, I was slightly primed for it. What now?

I had three months to find a job. A previous works colleague who now ran a company and a contractor whom I knew well had both previously requested I should contact them if ever I was looking for a new job. Well would you believe it they couldn't help me, strike them off my will. The BNF enquiry was bugging me, I had worked hard to get this, and I felt confident we had a reasonable chance of getting the order if we could produce the samples. The invoice value of the job was around £36,000.00 and I didn't want to let this go. The company were fully aware of the job but being aware and having the order were distinctly different. If they wanted to continue to sell the product would they give me the agency for the North? When I had found some months earlier the company who could produce the ceiling pads at a very competitive price, it seemed obvious there was a market for these, considering the only opposition was one other manufacturer at very uncompetitive prices.

If I could form a company to sell the ceilings and the pads would it be a viable propersition? I had never had the desire to go on my own or form a company, but this was an opportunity, and the value of the BNF contract would be a substantial start, plus I never like losing or giving up an order especially one of this size. I arranged a meeting with my company and asked them if I was to form a company would they give me the agency for the North. And they agreed subject to the financial backing and other assurances they would require. The choice was raising my own capital through a bank or finding a partner.

I approached the company who had originally given me the enquiry, they were not interested. I then contacted another contractor who I knew well. They were possibly the largest ceiling contractor in the northwest. I remember sitting in the meeting with them, it was between Christmas and New Year 1980, they were the most profitable and substantial ceiling contractor in the area. On the flipside I had a young family a mortgage and an uncertain future. Fourteen years later I had cause to remember that meeting. We discussed my proposal and they thanked me for considering them, but they were not interested.

Three years earlier, four fathers from the village where I lived had come together to save the disbanding of the local cub pack due to the leader retiring. I mentioned to Jack one of the four I had a proposition he may be interested in. He had quite a large accountancy practice and I knew he was involved with another business so we went after the Tuesday cub pack to slake our usual thirst. I told him of my situation and put my proposition to him about forming a company and would he be interested, and he was. We would each have a 50% share. He would provide and arrange the finance although I would have to put my house up as collateral. I could have an office in his premises and the facilities of the practice, I agreed. This was all very much dependent on my company agreeing and me securing the BNF order.

I arranged a meeting for the two of us with the MD and finance director. I had explained to Jack all the circumstances of the situation. He obviously wanted some assurance of the substance of the company and the reason they were getting rid of me was not my lack of ability. The meeting went well, and he was convinced that my dismissal was not through the lack of my ability, but to do with the lack of awareness and experience the company had in launching and marketing a new product, outside their normal market, and the company confirmed this. They were satisfied with our proposals and the financial guarantees we provided. The confirmation was done on a handshake with no formal agreement or contract. They would honour all orders we placed from the agreed area and appoint no other agent or supplier. There was no agreed time limit but an acceptance of let's see how it's goes in twelve months and we'll go from there. This may seem very fluid with no guaranteed assurances, but I had really no alternative, they were a well-respected company, and I had no evidence or hearsay that they would not honour their word. Then they produced the other good news the BNF samples were ready and we could pick them up now. We accepted their offer and the prospect of the BNF order to get the show on the road.

The contractor who had given me the enquiry was not interested in tendering for the job, so I approached another to install the mock-up and tender for the job that is of course presuming they accept the sample mock-up. They quickly installed it within a week. I then arranged for myself and Jack to visit the site and hopefully get their approval. This was a large complex and on arrival you had to register at the gatehouse. This was the first time I'd seen security police in a civilian situation carrying guns. We fulfilled the formalities and waited for our two contacts to arrive, which they very soon did. We exchanged the usual pleasantries, they said we would have to go in a car as the particular facility where the job was, was well inside the complex. They led the way out and went to the car parked next to the gatehouse. I went to the passenger door and one of our hosts to the driver's door, Jack and the other went to the back. We stood talking over the top of the car and each of us tried the doors which were locked. The man at the driver's door asked me if I had the key. 'No, I haven't got it,' I replied not understanding. 'Is this your car?' he says. 'No it's not mine,' I reply. 'Then whose is it?' 'I wouldn't know mine's over there in the parking lot,' when suddenly a man rushes out of the gatehouse exclaiming, 'Excuse me that's my car.'

We found the scenario put forward by our driver even more amusing. He said the guy must have parked there briefly while he went into the gatehouse. In that situation it's probable he would have left the car open with the keys still in the ignition. In which case 'I would have driven off' and goodness knows how that would have unfolded. He said when you went to the passenger door I presumed you thought being in the complex I should drive. We all found the incident amusing which was a good start as it made for a more relaxing situation.

The mock-up looked good. We removed a couple of the panels to assess the ease of access. They liked it and it answered their needs. They requested we submitted a price for the whole of the job and if it was within budget, they would send us the order. The contractor who installed the mock-up submitted a price and within a week received the order for the contract, and that demanded another night to slake our thirst. We were up and running, well forget the running. We had got the start we had hoped for it was a long road ahead.

CHAPTER NINE

Sink or Swim

The anxious wait for the order was over, but the anxious wait for the contract to be successfully completed had six weeks to run. This was only the second order produced, the first being my friend's shop and that was using a standard product with which an unexpected problem was found. This job was a hundred times bigger, a one off, with a specially made untested product. I must get some sleeping pills. The slaking of my thirst may be for different reasons if this goes pear-shaped, but it didn't, it ran like a dream, not a hitch, it was a great start.

I had a small office in Jack's premises. If I was out all messages were taken by reception and typing and letters were done by the secretary. Jack dealt with all the accounting and finance side leaving me free to do the selling. Having the use of Jack's secretary to type my letters was a great facility. Aside from the main purpose of this unintentionally it provided me with an intro into the entertainment industry. My letters I wrote by hand for Christine the secretary to type. The staff when gathered for lunch often used my misspelling for their entertainment and amusement, providing an alternative to the popular radio programme, 'Workers Playtime'. This might be a good fallback should things not work out.

After securing the order for BNF I had a meeting with the insulation converters whom I'd previously met when researching for the acoustic pads. They were keen to start the making of these, so we made a simple agreement, they make them we sell them. Their business and market was the thermal insulation industry, they had no connection with the ceiling market or the acoustic side. I gave them all the specifications for the various types of pads and with our margin added to their price we were still more competitive than the main and only supplier. We had simple literature produced and we circulated these to all the ceiling contractors throughout the UK.

This was 1981 how things have moved on in all aspects of the communication industry. I printed the address on the envelopes using a second hand 1850s (well it seemed like that, the British Museum took it off us in the end) manually operated addressing machine. Each individual address was on an embossed metal plate, these were stacked in a holding section. You placed the envelope on the flat bed, and as you brought the handle crashing down to create pressure, a plate slid under the envelope and hopefully resulted in the address being printed onto it. That is why my right arm is similar to Popeye's, but it did the trick, the enquiries started slowly coming in.

The acoustic pads placed on the back of the ceilings were generic. The type that was required was usually specified but not as a named product. The ceiling contractor could buy them from the ceiling manufacturer who in turn bought them from the only supplier of these pads whom I have previously referred to. They could also buy them direct from this supplier and that is what is known as a monopoly. With our prices below the other source of supply, we were enjoying increased enquiries and orders. Other than the manufacturing and the finances I did everything else. Processing enquires and orders, and occasionally when needed hiring a van and delivering the pads, although mainly we used outside transport.

One such delivery I made to London required three drops to three different sites. The last one of these I made at 5.30pm, it was to a national newspaper in the centre of London. The main entrance doors were closed, and I could see no one on reception. This was a multi storey building and there were lights showing in the third-floor windows. The only way I could think of to gain attention (before mobile phones) was to throw small stones at these. My aim was obviously good and faces appeared at the window. The windows didn't open so shouting was not an option, I therefore pointed to the main doors, with mannerisms indicating will you please open. They responded quickly, came down to reception and opened the doors. I carried the packs of pads in and left them stored in the reception. This was 1981 considering the increase in violent events bombings, gun and knife crime in the last decade. If this scenario was re-enacted in the present day, would the current occupants viewing a stranger throwing stones at the window, duly oblige by opening the doors, without hesitation or question, or would they air on the side of caution and phone the police? Who would have ever considered then we were living in more innocent times?

My main occupation was calling on contractors selling the pads, and architects gaining specifications for the ceiling system. An enquiry came in from the contractor who had installed the BNF job, they wanted a price on 8000 pads for a contract they had down south. I quoted them and we received the order, this was by far the largest order for pads we had received. Our supplier produced them, and they were dispatched. Large orders, particularly initial ones are exciting, thrilling, worrying and hopefully profitable. Especially for a small fledgling company when all the processes are still in their infancy. They can help to make you or break you, as established companies in the past have found out, and the phone call I received was going to put those facts to the test. The pads measured 60cmx60cmx2.5cm. They were made of a moderately dense mineral wool encased in flame retardant polythene. The polythene came in a tubular form. The mineral wool was inserted into the tube it was then cut and the two ends heat sealed making a tile size pad. The heat sealing was not sufficient, and the ends were opening, they would all have to be returned and resealed. SHIT. The cost of resealing them would have to be borne by our supplier. This also meant double transport which initially is our cost. The more worrying is the possible delay it could cause on the contract. This could have a knock-on effect for other trades. The possible cost can be considerable, and it does not take much consideration to implement these.

The 29th July 1981 everyone remembers that date, they don't? It was a national holiday. The reason, it was Charles and Dianna's wedding. The only people working were hospitals, police, and me, plus the bosses and staff of our supplier, and anybody else we could drag off the streets. The pads had arrived back the day before. We had to get them returned ASAP and we did. We started very early morning and finished just after the Police arrived at 2.30am the following morning. They had called wondering why the lights were on in the building. Well, why you're here do you mind helping with these last few packs into the container?' we asked jokingly with a hint of seriousness as our legs arms and other parts were on the point of collapse. With the speed we returned them combined with the holiday it caused the minimum of delay, and no contra charges. We considered sending Charles and Dianna a wedding present but there again they never sent us one.

Problems and mistakes are not the problem, it's how you deal and correct the problem that is the problem. You can't stop problems or things going wrong they will inevitably happen, you can reduce them through efficiency, but you will never completely eliminate them. You can though influence how they are addressed, and as a first test we did well and that was appreciated by the contractor, which gives them confidence and incentive, to place future business.

Business was increasing especially with the pads. Orders were coming in from all over the country especially from the south east. These were from contractors I didn't know, so I thought they deserved the honour of my calling. Although business was encouraging, our policy with expenses was to be thrifty. I had never abused my expenses with my past employers, and always stayed at reasonable hotels on visits away.

Where could I stay in London at a reasonable price, well I got one. A top-notch location in South Kensington, yes South

Kensington for£7.50. B&B beat that! Whatever I spent now was 50%of my money and I wasn't going over the top. Where might you ask would you get B&B in a central London prime location for that type of money? Well, I'll tell you, Baden-Powell House, the headquarters of the scout movement. Being a leader of a cub pack had its advantages. One problem however was how to drive the tent pegs into a wooden floor. I'm sure they'll have instructions 'Dib Dib Dob Dob' and all that, and stay I did. The only slight problem was the other two guys in the room, well that's camping, next time the Dorchester.

I would never want to live in London but what a great place to visit. Mind you having to be in at 7.30 and lights out at 8.00 in my accommodation was not appealing. It's a good job there was a window open, so I used my initiative badge to slip out to a Kensington local for a wee night cap. There I met an American chap leaning on the bar with whom I engaged in conversation of a kind. He quickly exemplified the phrase 'England and America two nations divided by a common language.'

'I love your two door cottages,' he says

'Two door cottages?' I reply

'Yes, your two door cottages,' he repeats.

'You mean like the ones in the country with thatch roofs?' I ask

'Yes, the black and white ones.'

'Black and white ones? Ah you mean Tudor,' I offer.

'Yes, the two door they're lovely.'

It's Time to climb back through the window.

Now come on lad you're in business, its business and more business, first and last, and in the day it was. I'd start early and finish late always squeezing in one last call. The reception I received was good. Office blocks construction was booming, and this was a major area for the insulation pads. It was unusual to have a rep call selling acoustic pads.

Contractors would just historically order from the well-known main supplier or the ceiling supplier. They were very receptive to a personal call and even more so to our lower prices. Not only were the orders increasing in numbers they were increasing in size and with different coverings depending on the application. I needed an assistant in the office and appointed a young girl of twenty who proved reliable and efficient. Well, we didn't want to get someone older who would have cost more. Some wag suggested we should change the company name to 'Tight& Tighter, it's still early days keep a steady ship.

We received an enquiry from the largest metal ceiling tile manufacturer in the UK. They purchased their pads from the main manufacturer of these the only manufacturer as I previously mentioned until we came on the scene. They had obviously heard of this upstart outfit up north. They requested if we could go and visit for a meeting. This was very encouraging to have the market leaders obviously interested in our product. There was a problem though which was twofold. We were now selling a metal ceiling, a different type and system to theirs but from their perspective it would be classed as competition. At this early stage they would not be aware of this. The other problem was we did not manufacture these pads ourselves. As a manufacturer they would not accept this. They would certainly soon find this out if we originally didn't tell them, and then they would go direct to our supplier.

I didn't know how many would be at this meeting and It was possible someone may know me or of me and my connection with my recent company and the ceiling system, it would be useful though to sound them out. The information they could provide could be as useful as what we could provide to them, I was uneasy though, so Jack volunteered to go. This was quite courageous considering he did not know anything in depth about the industry. It could prove to be counter productive if questions they asked he could not answer. I went through various things with him what to ask what to say. Wished him good luck and pushed him into the Lion's Den.

He returned certainly not a broken man but slightly bent. He said it was not to easy, he managed to get through but could not answer some of the questions and felt it was obvious he did not speak with the authority required for such a meeting, but he had left the door open for future discussions which in the not-too-distant future proved correct. His attending the meeting was very commendable and although it did not generate business it proved one thing of equal if not greater importance, his commitment to the company. Jack's accountancy business was very successful he had no need or dependency on our venture unlike me. It gave me assurance and confidence in our partnership and confirmed a very steadfast and valued partner.

Jack had many business contacts and clients. One we used was a graphic studio which produced our literature. Another was a client who assembled furniture within a unit in a 150-year-old rope works, which was still in operation. This was a two-storey building and the majority of the top storey was unused. He was looking out for another business for which to be involved and expressed an interest in making the pads we sold. Our current supplier was finding it difficult to offer the service we required with the increase in the business we were giving them. We arranged a meeting at the rope works. The building was fascinating and would have been best served turning into a tourist attraction. It looked as though it could have been producing rope since Trafalgar. It was around 120 metres long and twelve wide. The rope was produced in one piece down one side of the building it started at one end in hundreds of separate threads which were turned twisted and interwoven down the length of the building, fascinating, but nothing to do with our operation.

Jack introduced me to our prospective new supplier who appeared an amiable type of guy. We had brought samples of the products with the various coverings. I explained the specifications the quantities involved and the prices we would pay for them. He had a number of staff and was confident he could make them. We would supply all the materials and heat sealers. He would need to check the prices and would confirm within a couple of days his decision he ticked the boxes for us.

He conveyed a business attitude, and I was confident he could deliver the goods. He came back within two days and was happy with the prices and wanted to start ASAP. We ordered all the products required and he was in operation within two weeks. We now had two suppliers and over the next three months our new supplier was producing the majority of the orders.

Jack's meeting five months previous with the ceiling manufacturer was obviously not a lost cause. They contacted us and asked if they could visit us and have another meeting. We were now manufacturing ourselves so that obstacle had been removed. The meeting was with the head buyer and he duly arrived, he portrayed a slight air of dismissal or indifference, this was possibly engendered by representing the largest manufacture of their product in the country who could offer substantial business to a small two-bit supplier. We showed him round our manufacturing facility he asked the appropriate questions, and we offered the appropriate answers. We took him for lunch and we never saw him again. We did hear from them, they were not interested and then by grapevine a further comment –our manufacturing facility he best described as a hole in the wall. In Churchillian parlance, 'Some hole, some wall' as later years proved. And what of our potential customer and their premier position, they went into receivership some years ago.

Things were going very well perhaps too well considering we had only been in operation for nine months. The orders for the ceiling, although they tended to be small were quite good and the specifications were growing. We were receiving orders for the pads from contractors from all over the country, and I in turn was travelling throughout. And then I received the phone call. The rope works had completely burnt down during the night. I rushed over and was greeted with nothing that is nothing being left. It was a smouldering ruin. No walls just 120 metres of black, total burn out, everything that was combustible had combusted and things that were not had just collapsed. It was an unusual sight certainly from my inexperienced eyes of such matters. It covered the exact footprint of the building and there was only one thing left over one metre in height. The previous day we had a delivery of mineral wool which formed the core of the pads. This of course being incombustible was left standing measuring seven metres by three metres by three metres high, it stood as the sole survivor amid total devastation. A photograph should have been taken to demonstrate its fire-resistant qualities. I presume the length of the building acted like a tunnel, this combined with the interior wooden floors and beams soaked in oil from the rope making process, made for the perfect inferno, albeit not a towering one.

Now we had a problem. Thankfully our other supplier pulled out all the stops to cover the shortfall. We received some insurance from the owners of the building which was a slight compensation. Within a week we and our supplier Rob had found other premises, and these were superior to the previous ones. It was the ground floor of a small two storey mill. They were clean and spacious and we were in production within three weeks including new staff. Although our initial reaction to the fire was it would lead to disruption and possibly some loss of business, the reality was there was no significant loss.

Rob was now the only male at the new premises the rest therefore surprisingly all being female. This was no problem until the regular delivery by a forty-foot-long wagon arrived, full of packs of mineral wool. These were reasonably heavy, not pleasant to handle, caused by the irritation of the mineral fibre. The unloading demanded I put on my other hat of a general factotum, get changed and travel to the premises to assist Rob for two hours. This was all included in the pleasure of starting a business. It's a good job I'd developed strength in my right arm from the previously described operation of the addressing machine.

Business was flourishing, including the ceiling system, in the first year of having the agency we had a turnover of £86,000 just for the ceilings, for the second year we enjoyed a similar turnover. This was in contrast to my eighteen-month full time employment with the company when I'd received one small order for my friend's new shop. This was the consequence of the specifications I had obtained when working for them and new orders since starting the company. They were pleased and I think a little surprised, even though I had made them fully aware of the potential orders. In fact, they were so pleased they took the agency off us and decided to sell the ceilings once again direct themselves. Fortunately, the turnover from the pads was now sufficient to sustain the company, although losing the ceiling business was not welcome, it was satisfying to know the success we had enjoyed had reversed their policy.

Our success with the pads had obviously not gone unnoticed by our only competitor. We were taking large jobs away from them which previously they would have automatically obtained. Contractors would report to us of their annoyance when they found out they had lost an order. The two main metal tile manufacturers were also losing pad orders to us, they purchased these from the main pad supplier, and it was a loss of revenue for them. Their growing concern was demonstrated one morning when I called at the Mill. There outside viewing the premises was my old nemesis who, thirteen years previously had been offered the job by my old boss with the French company, which, when he had turned it down I was offered it. Good morning Jim, I expressed with a look of surprise which he mirrored. I had met him on a few occasions since his decision which launched me on my new career. On refusing that offer he had taken a rep's job with a metal tile manufacturer, with which he was still employed. I could see he was slightly taken aback by this unexpected meeting, demonstrated by his slightly stuttering incoherent vocabulary. Once he had regained his limited eloquence, he could only offer the truth. His boss had asked him to go and look at this company who were nicking all these pad orders from them. We enjoyed a bit of a chuckle, he seemed very relaxed about it, with an attitude of 'so what.' I thought it best to be prudent and not to ask him inside after all he might then be impressed. Better for him to report back, it looks like a bit of a tin-pot company working in a hole in the wall, here today gone tomorrow.

The very nature of his presence confirmed the reports we had received. Was this good or was this bad, should we be pleased or concerned. Should our success continue would they just ignore it, I doubt it. This was the first competition they had experienced with the pads, so their reaction was untested. Well, there's nothing we can do certainly at the moment other than be aware.

CHAPTER TEN

The Party's Over

The current premises which Rob rented were proving too small. The mineral wool which the pads were made from was very bulky. It required a large area for storage. We decided we needed larger premises. Rob had proved very efficient with the manufacturing of the pads and he was now our sole supplier. Should he decide for whatever reason to move on to other things we would be left high and dry, we asked him therefore if he wished to join the company as a director. Jack and I would retain the major shareholding, but it would give him an involvement and security and in addition to ourselves.

We found suitable premises close by these were half the ground floor area of a once large cotton mill. It included a huge loading bay which would house the largest lorry. We retained all the staff (these were all women) and all involved with the actual making of the products. One in particular Kath, who had the unofficial title of works manager or supervisor was over all the women and ran the manufacturing with great efficiency. She had been with the company from the time we had moved into the previous premises. In future years she became a very deserving director of the company and its longest serving employee. Rob also employed two teenage lads, these were engaged in the loading the lifting and the physical necessities of a manufacturing process.

I now moved from my office in Jacks premises to one of the two we had built in the new unit for Rob and me. Very soon after moving in a neighbour of Jacks who worked for BNF (a different division from the ceiling we installed) mentioned to him they needed large cylinder blankets to go round cylinders to control the temperature within them. Was this something we could produce? We arranged the customary meeting to establish their requirements and concluded we could make them. They measured 150x60x10cm thick. We found an ideal flame-retardant plastic-coated fabric which encased the mineral wool core. Sewn to the fabric were ties which secured them to the cylinder. They liked our prototype, and we received the order. This was a large contract worth around £60,000. We purchased a second-hand industrial sewing machine and employed an experienced women sewer to make them just for the duration of the contract. The contract went well, and the profit was a welcome addition to our normal operation.

The pads were still selling well but we were experiencing for the first-time competition from the opposition. They had obviously decided action was needed to combat the decline in their business. A contractor would ring for a price I would quote him, and he would inform me, he could get it for less than the figure I had given him. It was then a decision to match it or better it. This was happening in the minority of calls, but it was growing. A contractor may just accept your price without indicating they had a better one, therefore you were left wondering. This obviously was a new experience and a concern; I was not keen on getting involved with a Dutch auction every time an enquiry came in. The additional underlying concern was our competitor the main UK producer of the pads. They were a much larger company than we were and the pad business was the much smaller part of their operation. They could if they wished offset this for a period against the larger side until they had seen us off, and their determination over time would have succeeded, but for the saving grace of two hours.

The strategy of the opposition was speculation on our part, they may not want to get into a slanging match themselves, but I doubted it. They had held court for many years, and I did not think they would relinquish it easily. To provide a cushion against possible serious competition I suggested to my co-directors we should open a ceiling showroom to sell suspended ceilings to the public and small businesses. My main career had been in the business and I knew it well. There was a growing market for suspended ceilings in the home, in kitchens and bathrooms. There were two suppliers of ceilings in the area to the domestic market; one was a branch of a company in the southeast, the other was a longstanding friend of mine (well he was at the moment) who had a joinery business. We built a showroom displaying the ceilings and bought in a small stock. The most popular for domestic use was the illuminated type and the main manufacturer of this type was only a mile away which was very convenient. In addition, the husband of one of the women who worked for us was a ceiling fixer which was even more convenient. We could therefore offer a supply and fix service. We put an advert in the local papers and the response was encouraging. Rob or myself if I was in the office served the customers and over the following month there was a steady flow of sales.

An incident occurred within a couple of months of opening which was a precursor for more serious future events. Rob assisted by Kath made the wages up in the showroom for the twenty-five women we employed. This in retrospect was not a good place to do this and why he did it here was foolish. On this occasion a man rushed into the showroom hit Rob knocked over Kath and made off with the money. They testified it happened so quickly they could do nothing to stop it. The thief knew exactly what he was doing. The police suspected that it was an inside job, and this ultimately proved the case. The area we were in was certainly not one of the wealthier areas of the town, and had a reputation that would not have adorned Mother Teresa's CV. Nothing could be proved we just needed to stay vigilant. Not only were we feeling the pressure from increased competition, but we also now had to accommodate the threat of the local crime syndicates. Where might I ask had the carefree, crime free, in fact everything free, times of Paris and Rotterdam gone?

We received a visit by a representative from large foam manufacturers. He had heard we produced acoustic products and they manufactured an acoustic foam which he thought would be of interest to us, and it was. The problem with the pads they were a generic product which could be made by anyone. The foam the representative offered had an open cell structure which could absorb sound. It was black, flame retardant and came in rolls. This was ideal to put over the back of open cell suspended ceilings and it was not marketed to the ceiling industry, I liked it. We could have it tested over a ceiling to give performance figures and offer it as a named product, and this we did we called it 'Coustifoam'. This meant it could be specified by name and would have to be purchased direct from ourselves. We produced a single page leaflet and samples and circulated them to the trade. We had at last, a product of our own. In addition, it also gave substance to the company that we specialised in acoustic insulation for suspended ceilings. The response was moderate but encouraging. This product may not be the making of us but it's a start.

The suspended ceiling side was slowly growing. We were doing more supply and fix jobs. These were only small but profitable. We only worked direct for a client we never did subcontract work for a builder. On the pad side the competition was gaining in intensity and making these less profitable. We were receiving around the same number of orders but at lower value, having to match or lower what the competition had offered. I was convinced by their pricing and the reports I was hearing they were deliberately trying to break us. Something had to give. We had to cut our costs our overdraft with the bank was growing. Jack and I decided Rob had to go. The manufacturing ran well, we had a stable workforce of twenty-five women and four teenage lads ran by Kath the supervisor. I would have to oversee the works along with the selling and all else. It was not pleasant telling Rob we offered him some compensation and his car and a couple of months salary. He was not happy but had to accept it.

CHAPTER ELEVEN

The Awakening

When a company is formed its founding directors or partners are generally persons who have experience in the business, trade, or profession of the company they are forming, in my case that was the selling of suspended ceilings. My experience was not with insulation and certainly not with manufacturing. Many are started with two people offering their expertise in two of the main functions selling and manufacturing. I only have to mention Rolls and Royce, who were reasonably successful by bringing the two main ingredients to the table. I was now the one-man band in selling, marketing, manufacturing, procurement, recruitment bad debt chasing, and making my own cup of tea.

The next twelve months were to prove the most stressful, pressurised and experience forming in my working life. Rob had been directly in charge of all the operatives, directing, instructing, and keeping his finger on the pulse. He had employed people over the years in a working environment and had considerable experience, I hadn't, plus he was involved with the manufacturing on a day to day basis I wasn't. Eighty percent of my time was spent on selling and marketing. I would get involved as needed, and to an extent the works ran itself with the experienced operatives. The women were no problem, the lads proved different.

The first experience occurred within the first three weeks of my multi-occupational position. A colleague of Jacks asked if he could leave his car in the loading bay for a couple of nights while away on business. He left the keys so I could move it when required. On arriving to work on the second morning the car wasn't there. I asked around and of course no one knew any reason why it should be missing. I called the police, and they interviewed all the staff. Two of the lads had got the keys from my office and had taken it out for a joy ride at night while they were working. Crashed it, luckily not badly, and left it. These two lads had been with us for some time. They were good workers obliging and respectful. We had allowed them on occasions to stay on at night to finish a job which was due for delivery the following day. I or Rob would call to lock up at a given time. They had always done a good job there had been no reason to doubt them. The police charged them. They apologised and asked if I would not sack them but give them another chance. The area we were in was poor and did not have a good reputation. I, naively, had sympathy for them aware of the environment they lived and mixed in. Other than this incident they had proved reliable and reasonable workers. I allowed them to stay.

Some time prior to this incident another lad we employed when Rob was with us stood out with his personality and demeanour. He lived very close to the works and would tell us of the pressure put on him by his brothers and peers to get involved in some theft or law-breaking activity. This provided an insight into the mindset and social normality of many in the local community. We had arranged to have, for a week in one of the large DIY stores, a small exhibition stand for the ceilings. This was to be manned alternatively by Rob and myself. We asked him if he would like to join us. He jumped at the opportunity. This allowed him the experience to use, probably for the first time, his personality and ability for his own fulfilment. And the experience gave him the confidence to apply for a sales position in one of the national electrical retailers, which he got. We were very pleased for him even though we lost a very good employee. He had escaped the social norm and advanced himself against the odds. To most people this perhaps was nothing special, I believe for him it was a great achievement and one he should have been proud of, a knight hood would not have been out of place.

The two joy riders returned to work after their court appearance in quite an upbeat mood. The amount they had been fined they seemed to feel was a let off. I certainly did not want them or expect them to be sent down. But I did not like the rather jocular dismissive manner which they thought of their sentence. Whether this served as a deterrent, time would tell.

Not dismissing the two lads may have served the impression with all four of them that I was a soft touch. There may have been a slight element with this as I had been brought up on the other side of town, in a working-class area, but in a better working-class area. The area was made up on the whole of decent privately owned terraced houses. When I was eighteen, I was around a similar age to these lads. There was certainly no undercurrent of crime in the area and I did not know of anyone who was involved or had been involved with the police or crime.

The place where our mill was situated was in a council estate. Now there are good and bad council estates, and even good and not so good areas within the same estate. The bad areas are indicative of a ghetto, which in social terms means there's no or little chance of escape. I had, within this period while we were in the mill, parents coming to see me asking if I would reemploy their sweet little cherub, who I'd either sacked or who had been taken into custody for questioning. I would suggest to them had they ever thought of moving from the area to give their offspring and themselves a better chance, invariably they hadn't. It is a downward spiral that insights crime and little hope, but it did provide a broadening of my education.

My ability in the expertise and handling of employees may be questionable. I trusted the same could not be said of my competence in sound insulation. My office was situated near the entrance at one end of the unit but within the whole of the manufacturing area. It was constructed of timber studding and plaster board. One of the processes demanded in the manufacture was the spraying of glue onto the pads. This was done by a spray both with good air extract which was positioned at the extreme end of the unit from my office. There were four women required on this process and being the jolly lot they were, they would sing to entertain themselves and everybody else. As the process progressed with a little aid from the small residue of glue, the volume increased. Now closer to my office another process was being enacted were the operatives preferred the radio. This inevitably was some head banging rendering which they had instructions to keep the volume low. Unfortunately as the glue songsters increased in volume, to combat this, so did the radio. Now, no matter how effective our insulation was a six-foot-thick concrete wall would not stop this volume and as this crescendo reached its climax often my phone would ring. I could hardly hear the voice on the other end saying something about they had a noise problem. I would excuse myself put the phone on the desk close the door go outside and shout 'Turn that bloody radio down' return to telephone and say, 'Sorry about that now you were saying you had a noise problem?' It's an old cliché the house that needs decorating is often a decorator's. Obviously my expertise needed expanding on two fronts.

The felonious deeds of one or more of our happy little band of felons, was still active. We had large rolls of aluminium foil large enough to cook all the turkeys bred by Bernard Matthews (who's old enough to remember him?) occasionally one would go missing. How and by whom I could never find out. The four proved the fact there was no trust among thieves. One lost his wage packet, he was convinced it had either been stolen or he'd possibly dropped it, and it had been found by one of the other three lads, who'd then conveniently doubled his wage for that week. I questioned them all with no success.

Not long after this episode one of our regular deliveries of mineral wool arrived. They came en masse to my office demanding more money to unload it. It was a two-hour heavy operation and one they had done many times before as part of their job. It is known as having you over a barrel, and it certainly would be difficult and tiring to unload it on my own, although I would have asked for the women's help. I refused and threatened them with dismissal. They backed down and carried out the task. This along with other incidents was certainly the last straw. I'd had enough they were going but I'd have to choose the time, but that was not to be before the biggest incident of all.

Since the wages snatch from the showroom, they had been made up at Jack's offices. These were then kept locked in Rob's old office until they were paid. This had an outside wall to the street. It had two windows which were three metres above ground level. There was a crash of glass from the office and Kath the supervisor unlocked the door rushed in and saw a man balanced on the windowsill with one leg through the window. She tried to grab his leg, but he jumped down to the pavement. She looked through the window and recognised him. He occasionally at lunch break would meet and chat with one of the lads in the entrance. The police obtained the name of the intruder from our own suspected informant who denied any involvement. What intelligence does it take to realise if he'd been seen meeting the suspected robber on our premises, he would be the prime suspect for the informer? Why didn't he just meet him around the corner, bang goes his promotion. They soon found his address and I'm sure they knew of him. He was charged with breaking and entering and attempted robbery. To slightly compound this situation on my first meeting with the police they had asked the names of the four lads. One of these I had put in charge of the others, not in an official way but more to make decisions, if needed. He was quite bright and assertive. When I mentioned his name, they both looked at each other. 'Is there a problem' I asked. 'Well let's put it this way' they replied. 'Do you remember the smash and grab last year in Market Street?' I nodded. 'Well let's just say he was in the car.' And with that I cancelled my 'Worldly Wise' credit card, well, I never used it anyway.

The case hinged round Kath's evidence and her recognition of the suspect. She would be required to go to court to give evidence and confirm her recognition. A few days after the suspect had been charged, word came back from the suspect via our suspected (sorry guilty beyond all reasonable, unreasonable and any other type of doubt there may be) informant. That should she give evidence against him she would be dealt with. That was it. He was out of the door quicker than a rat up a drainpipe. I informed the police of this threat and they acted on it. Intimidating a witness is a very serious offence. Kath was determined to go through with it. I accompanied her on the day of the trial. The defendant had family and friends in the court making it very intimidating, but she was resolute. She gave her evidence with clarity and efficiency. He was sentenced and sent down.

After I had sacked the informant, I received a phone call a couple of weeks later from a representative of the unfair dismissals board or whatever body it was. He advised me that our informant friend had made out a case for unfair dismissal and could he come and see me. We made an appointment and he arrived and knocked on my office door. I said, 'Come in.' He did, and I greeted him with 'Hello Len' and he replied, 'Hi Eddie well that's a surprise' and so it was, we knew each other. I explained the whole sordid details and he departed saying, 'Just leave it with me.' And that was the last I heard about it. This I may add was nothing to do with who you know, but more to do with what you know. There was a final epilogue thirty-two years later to this particular event. I called at a builder's merchant to buy a product they had ordered for me. The man at the counter had to go into the office to check on the delivery. While I had been talking to him a suited well-dressed man had stood a few feet away at the back of the counter. He looked at me and said 'I worked for you years ago.' I looked at him with no recognition. 'How many years ago'? I asked. 'In the eighties' he replied, 'Sorry I don't recognise you, what's your name?' Jack Bannister he replied our long-ago informant. He'd recognised my name. He appeared to have done well and credit to him.

Just as I was enjoying what appeared a little good fortune I was brought back to earth with an even greater crash. Soon after these recent events, Kath, who was always punctual, had not come in this particular morning. She hadn't given any reason the previous day why she would be late. Around 11am there was a knock on my door, and she entered. Dressed it appeared for an audience with the queen. 'Can I see you?' she asked. She apologised for being late and then informed me she had been for an interview with the premier department store in the town and had been offered the job of a manager over one of the departments. She apologised for this, knowing the position it would leave me in, but had accepted it, and I couldn't blame her. She was far more capable than the job she held with us and I was certain she would be ideal in it. I wished her well overcoming my disappointment which I am sure she observed. I couldn't think of any one of the current employees who would automatically take her place, getting someone equally capable would not be easy. My initial thought was I would have to wear another hat and become more hands on, certainly for the time being, this was the last thing I wanted. At 12.05, I remember the time, there was a knock on my door, and she entered again, 'I've been thinking' she said, 'I've decided to stay.' A decision which in time she would be rightfully rewarded being made a director of the company and its longest serving employee, as for the department store that finished trading some years ago.

CHAPTER TWELVE

Action

I was a slow learner, too patient and too soft, but not anymore. The three remaining lads had to go. The concern was how to do it. Do I get rid of them one by one or altogether, whichever way there may be some reaction. They had to go immediately on telling them. I decided for better or worse they'd go all together. On my way to work on the day of their dismissal my mind was obviously on the forthcoming act. Turning right at a junction I cut in front of a police motor cyclist causing him to swerve. The siren and blue light went on immediately, I stopped, and he parked in front of me. I got out of the car approached him and apologised, followed by a tirade of words explaining where I was going and the task I was about to perform. Calm down, he said, and he spent five minutes advising me on the best course of action, including putting my car out of the way. (This officer was too nice to book anyone.) I thanked him and I approached the oncoming task with a little more assurance. I called the three into my office told them they were being dismissed immediately and the reasons why. Warned them the police had their names and should there be any repercussions they would act accordingly especially after the recent events.

The police had never offered any such response, but it sounded plausible in the current climate. They left grudgingly but without any problem. I had parked my car well round the back of the mill, obviously not well round enough, it had been covered in cement dust, I was able to remove this causing no damage. I was actually grateful for this considering the damage they could have inflicted. I must remember to send them a thank you card. During the following week, the mother and father of the lad who I'd given the small promotion to, and who was also the smash and grab accomplice, came to see me. They requested if I would consider taking him back. 'Taking him back where?' I responded. I offered a little sympathy to their wish and concern, but my days of social consideration and empathy were long gone.

The experience of the latter months was certainly outside my working experience. My job and priority was the sales. The job of running or overseeing the works and manufacturing was thrust upon me due to Rob leaving. Kath was very capable and did an excellent job of running the day-to-day manufacturing, and I left that with her. I perhaps had a slightly detached attitude and not the commitment and hands on approach that was needed. It was an intrusion or interruption to my main job. The employment of the lads had not been my responsibility they were there when I took over, and they had been the main problem. Perhaps I was a soft touch which they exploited. I didn't run a tight enough ship and due to the nature of selling I would be out or away. In the well-known song from Oliver 'I think I better think it out again.'

The priority was to get replacements for the lads. I decided two would be enough and contacted the job centre. An applicant came the following day. He must have felt he was being interrogated by MI6. I resisted asking how far his ancestry goes back and did he have any known villainous descendants. But I did ask him had he a record (and I didn't mean by Elvis) this in 1986 was against the law. Ironically you had to break the law to find if those you were employing had up held it. Did I hear someone say the law is an ass? He hadn't or so he said. He was in his late twenties and he appeared to tick all the boxes. He was on board, start tomorrow. The following day another captain of industry arrived. He was in his early twenties and very smartly dressed. I went through the same interrogation and he admitted he had a police record.

'What for' I asked
'Robbery,' was his reply
'Where?' I enquired
'I don't know it was dark.'
'Where about was it?' I asked him
'Round here somewhere.'
'How long ago was it?'
'About nine months,' he informs me
'What did you steal?'
'I think a drill, tools radio, office things.'
'When you say tools was it a quite large red toolbox?' I enquired.

He looks at me a sudden realisation on his face.

'It was here, you stole from us you little_ _ _ _ _'

He didn't get the job. They had entered via windows in the loading bay round the back of the mill this was a large, cavernous dark area at night. He had arrived today from the street into the showroom with no obvious resemblance. He may also have stolen the aluminium rolls, although I doubted that. And all along the lads were innocent, I'll coco.

A third candidate arrived. He was in his mid-thirties and lived just across the way from the mill. No excuse for him to be late for work. I went through the now standard procedure and he appeared as innocent and as pure as the driven snow. This I assessed having just reapplied for my 'Worldly Wise' credit card. The two new recruits proved to be good workers reliable and trustworthy. Don't speak to soon my lad. And so it proved to be until after around nine months Eric our mid-thirties operative didn't turn up one morning. He can hardly be late for work, so I went across the road to see him. He had just got up or perhaps had never been to bed. The night before he and a mate had gone into town on their way home they passed a Labour Club with conveniently a window left open. So, as you would in such circumstances when an opportunity was presented to you to satisfy your still raging thirst, they climbed through and helped themselves to the free bar. When the police arrived, they would not believe their mitigation having been locked in, believing more the story they had been observed climbing through the window. They requested to be charged with just entering as there was no breaking involved due to the window being open. The more revealing testament was he had decided not to bother coming back to work again because he could get nearly as much on the social as we paid him. How did we lose the Empire?

And now there was one and he was good, reliable and a good worker. We needed another so I asked Michael my eldest son. He had just left sixth form and was on the long summer holiday and waiting to go to University. He mainly operated the large saw and was very efficient. Work experience and some pocket money would prove very useful. At last, we had some stability. The foam supplier introduced to us another of their products. This was a sound barrier blanket. It had a lead core sandwiched between two layers of foam, the same foam we purchased from them. This was ideal as an acoustic curtain hung within a ceiling void. It would reduce the sound travelling though the void. Again, like the other product we bought from them it was not used in our industry. We named it 'Soundstop' tested it, leafleted it and sold it. This gave us two named specifiable products which were our own. The pads were experiencing more competition and we were getting fewer orders for them. The ceiling sales and the supply and fix side were steady and the two new products we had of our own would take time to get established in the market.

We decided as things may be looking up to open a Yorkshire office. Just before we had formed the company in 1981 we had purchased, along with Gwens' two sisters and family, a static caravan which the three families shared. This was in a small market town in the Yorkshire Dales. Over the next few years it proved of great benefit for holidays and weekend retreats, which owing to financial restraints and work pressure were in short supply. When I took a week's holiday or a few days at the caravan I would ask my cousins husband a retired manager in the cotton industry, if he would man the office and keep an eye on the place while I was enjoying myself. I would then phone in every morning at 9.30 from the office we had close to the caravan site. This was unfortunately very small around six square feet commonly known as a telephone kiosk. To make one call to the office was easy unfortunately the consequences of the call necessitated me then making others, and may be some from the previous day. Fortunately some time earlier BT had brought out phone cards which eliminated the prior need of a pocket full of coins. But the facility of the phone card had no assistance in the balancing act of the papers I had, or writing on the small shelf improvised as a desk. This difficult procedure could be then compounded by the arrival of another potential occupant who wished to use the facility of my office. I would gather up the papers exit and hope the new occupant would not be on some long-distance call to family in America. I tried to make this daily procedure as little disruptive to the holiday as possible. It did cause amusement to visiting friends when I told them of my Yorkshire office, pointing out the kiosk as we drove past.

We have a lot to thank the Edinburgh born Scottish scientist Alexander Graham Bell for as the inventor of the telephone, and many people of course know that. But we have possibly even more to thank the Edinburgh born Scottish scientist James Clerk Maxwell for, his theory of electromagnetism was fundamental in the development of the mobile phone, and not many people know that. Mobiles were brought out in the mid-1980s'. Had they done so two years earlier I would not have required the Yorkshire office, and even fewer people know that.

Enough with theory back to practicalities. I hadn't had a pay rise for three years and things on the personal finances as well as the company were tight. I decided to go and see my friendly bank manager. I had a small overdraft, and it would help if I could increase it. The company used another bank so the assistant manager whom I'd never met knew nothing of my personal situation. On explaining it to him he understood it, but obviously did not appreciate it. He replied and expressed in a very meaningful way, 'Can you not live within your means?' the words echo to this day. I'd obviously got the unfriendly manager. I'd filled him in fully with my situation, but I felt filling him in with my right hand would have been more satisfying, but less productive for my request. He reluctantly granted me an increase of £1000. Thank you I said, I'll call again if I need more.

I had never seen this manager before in my life. A week after my meeting with him I was with my wife in our local supermarket. In the trolley on top of the groceries I'd put a bottle of whisky and also one of gin. On turning into an aisle, who should be coming up the other way pushing a trolley but my ever so friendly bank manager. Where the hell has he come from thinks I. Now the two bottles of the hard stuff fully exposed on the top may not be the best thing to confront him with, considering he has just granted me £1000 for survival and to live a frugal life. So, I turn around sharp-like, and deposit both back from whence they came. My wife wondering what the hell I was playing at. I wait until I see him exit the check out and return to collect my ill-gotten booty. It looks as though this guy may have some influence on my drinking habits for the foreseeable future. If he thinks he can make me teetotal he can think again.

I had the last say all be it many years later. I never had the pleasure of meeting him again face to face since my overdraft request, although I had recognised him from a distance a couple of times over the passing years in the supermarket. (Doesn't he go anywhere else?)The company fortunes along with mine had now changed for the good. So much so rather than me requesting an overdraft from the bank they were now inviting me to the Open Golf Championship. Unfortunately, my friend was no longer there to share in my good fortune. It was Christmas and where else would I be at this time of year but in my local supermarket? And my trolley was overflowing with the liquid hard stuff, soft stuff and every kind of alcoholic wrapping in between. I was in a queue at the checkout when lo and behold who should come next to me in the adjoining queue but yes, my friend the reluctant overdraft grantor. And there in his trolley was one, yes one lone bottle of sherry. Now I am sure he would not recognise me after all this time, but should I refresh his memory, yes. So, I asked him, 'Its Mr Graham isn't it?'

He looked at me with a questioning expression, 'Yes he replied'

'You won't remember me we met many years ago when I requested an increase in my overdraft, and you asked me why I couldn't live within my means,'

'Oh,' slightly apprehensively he replied.

'Well, I'm pleased to see you are living within yours,' pointing to his bottle of sherry, 'and you'll be pleased to know I'm now also living within mine,' indicating my trolley.

And with that, I left him to indulge in his little treat.

Now back to the plot. Luck plays a part in all our lives at certain times and situations, be it good or bad. Perhaps bad is remembered more because after all no one wants that. The events that followed were of the good variety, if they had been of the alternative my life would have taken a different course.

Along with my personal overdraft the company had a far bigger one. Should the company go into liquidation the debts would be shared between Jack and myself. Jack had arranged all the finances for forming the company and I had signed my house over as collateral. The overdraft over the last twelve months had steadily increased. It was a Monday morning 9.30am the day and time are etched on my mind, and Jack phoned me. The bank had been on and unless we got £15,000 into the account to reduce the overdraft by a deadline of 1 pm they would call in the facility, which meant close us down. Now where do you get £15,000 at 9.30 on a Monday morning? Although it would not be pleasant for Jack, he had other properties and far more assets than me. I'd better start looking how much a tent cost.

Over the previous two weeks we had installed the largest ceiling contract we had undertaken. This was for a privately owned engineering company. They made components for BAC and needed a suspended ceiling in a part of one of their factories. The value was around £20,000. On the Friday the end of the previous week the job had been completed. When I had first gone to measure the job, I had met the owner and Managing Director, and he stated as soon as you have finished the job, I will pay you. This was unusual in that although you expect to be paid it is not necessarily directly on completion. It would usually take between two to four weeks, on any contract, and certainly one the size of this. It would need first to be inspected, and normally there would be a small amount of snagging required. This had only been finished on the Friday one working day before.

This was the only possible source to obtain the money. I had to receive it and get it into the bank within three hours. The possibility of that seemed virtually impossible. When he said I'll pay you when you have finished it, he certainly would not mean within two hours of me requesting it. When I phoned him, what is the chance of him being in? He could be away on business. He could be in a meeting. He could say I'm busy today come tomorrow. He could say I've not had chance to look at it yet. All these options were very probable, and completely reasonable. I phoned him and was put through to his personal secretary, who in turn put me through. I told him we had finished the job on Friday, of which he was aware, and said he had promised to pay us as soon as the job was finished 'Yes, that's right,' he confirmed, 'come and get the cheque.'

Truly amazing, what are the chances of that happening? Fate, luck, good fortune, unprecedented is another word. At the time we needed the money so quickly, that all the elements should come together to provide it was truly amazing. In addition to those I've already mentioned, it was fortunate we got the contract. It was fortunate that initially I saw the MD and not a manager, or someone over maintenance. They would not have had the authority to offer payment so quickly. It was fortunate we had finished the job on the Friday. Should any of these probabilities have arisen I would not have secured the cheque. I would probably have lost my house and suffered life changing circumstances. But I did secure it, and I can look back on this period and appreciate fate, luck and good fortune where on our side in great abundance.

The decision to start selling and installing ceilings was taken as an interim to support the main business. It was made with vision and anticipation for the future. The decision was positive and proactive. It created the framework that enabled all the elements to come together that saved the company. Was it lucky they did so? You bet it was. On the other hand, you have got to buy a ticket before you can win the lottery.

On a little lighter note, Rob our ex-director had always been interested in alternative medicine and osteopathy. A far cry you may add from suspended ceilings and insulation. When he had left, he set up a local clinic and went into it full time. A friend of his used to call occasionally delivering to us. He told me Rob was doing quite well had nice premises and regular clients. He said he was treating one patient not long after he had left us. The man was lying on the bed and said looking up at Rob 'You seem familiar I seem to recognise your face.' Rob couldn't think why, never treating him before. The man after a time repeated this again. Rob again could offer no reason and continued gently administering his osteopathic skills, when suddenly the man said, 'I know you sold me a suspended ceiling.' Rob's response was asking him 'just to relax or this might hurt a little.'

The acoustic insulation continued to be the main business, but we would not have survived without the contribution provided by the ceiling business. It was the ceilings that had saved us, they had proved our saviour. It was never my intention to become a ceiling contractor these were the companies we supplied with the sound insulation. You can't be a competitor to them and with the other hand expect them to buy from you. We needed to cut our overheads.

The gatehouse to the mill had become vacant. This was a single storey building on the other side of the mill gates. It was the administrative building when the mill was in operation. I enquired, and it was available at a considerably lower rent than our current premises. Over the last year I had met two companies who were insulation converters. They could produce the acoustic pads for us, just as we had previously operated before we started to manufacture ourselves. My plan was to stop manufacturing and sell off all the machinery, and for these two companies to manufacture the pads for us. We would obviously work on a lower margin, but this would be offset by lower overheads. We would have our own two special named products and the ceilings all operating on the same margins. Two of us could run this as against the twenty-five we now employed. I asked Kath our works manager if she would be interested in being a team of two, and she was. I would be out 50% of the time and she would cover the telephone sales, ordering and deliveries to name but three. She would be fully capable of this I was confident, and she soon proved me correct.

The unfortunate consequence of this decision I had to make the remaining staff of twenty-four women and now one man redundant, never a pleasant job. They took it well and as in the past any excuse for a knees-up would not be missed. They had been an excellent work force and I couldn't deny them one last fling. Apart from that I may enjoy it. A basic business principle for a successful business is business before pleasure. Mine has tended to err on the side of pleasure before business, need I say more. And this final fling produced one amusing episode. We arranged it at a well-known restaurant. This was a converted 200-year-old large stable block of a sixteenth-century hall. The women were a lively bunch who knew how to enjoy themselves on a night out, especially when it was on the house. Time shot by. All the other diners and guests had left but our merry little band of well soused operatives had no intention of doing so at least not voluntarily.

The manager had requested in a nice but then a never-increasing stern request to leave. Jack and I were doing the same. Then some would go missing, others were enjoying flirting with the waiters although they were not reciprocating. It would have been easier quelling a jail riot. Eventually we got them out about an hour after closing. Now this building had a large courtyard. You left the restaurant walked through the courtyard and then out through the main arched stone entrance, which still had the original large three-inch-thick oak doors. We had arranged for taxis and a minibus to pick us up. To get the women into the appropriate vehicle was proving equally as difficult. While all this was happening the manager had come out locking the restaurant and now closing and locking with a little difficulty the two huge oak doors. He went past Jack and me on his way to his car. We offered a good night and a sorry he offered nothing, not even a glance. Obviously, he'd had enough of our generous custom. The women were virtually all in the taxis when someone shouted, 'Has any one seen Maggi?' So, we checked the bus and three taxis, but no Maggi.

'She must still be inside.'

'She can't be.'

The conclusion was, she was still inside.

'Oh my God'

'What do we do?'

'There's a car coming down from the car park it must be the manager,' Jack observed. 'We better stop him'

'I'm not stopping him,' I courageously volunteered.

And Jack stepped forward with hand outstretched.

He stopped wound the window down glared, 'Yes?' said with intent.

'We think one of the women is still inside,' stated Jack

He got out of the car never said a word. He didn't need to, his demeanour said it all. There'd be no small talk here. He unlocked the oak doors and walked with purpose across the courtyard Jack and me following in his wake. He unlocked the restaurant door into reception and we immediately heard it, the gentle sob. We entered the dining hall and there sitting at a table in total darkness was Maggi. She had gone to the ladies and was left in ink blackness to consider her fate. Knowing

Maggi, her sobbing was nothing to do with being left, more to do with she hadn't got the key to the bar. We escorted her to the bus, and she climbed aboard to the strains of 'One young lady locked in a lavatory,' a most appropriate rendition, which certainly would not have been appreciated by the manager. Who had stormed off in a huff, or it could have been a Toyota?

CHAPTER THIRTEEN

Small is Best

After a little renovation of the new premises my youngest son Mark and the son of friends helped with the move. All the machinery had been sold so it was mainly desks and office equipment that needed carrying a short distance to our new abode. From the main door you walked into a hall. To the left was a kitchen to the right a small room. The hall led into the main room. This is where Kath had her desk and we made it into a showroom by installing a suspended ceiling displaying the different types we sold. To the left of this was a small room which I made my office and to the back of the main room where two further quite large rooms we could use for storage. Perfect hopefully, and certainly a far cry from half the ground floor of a former cotton mill which we had vacated. It formed a tight and hopefully very manageable operation. I could now concentrate on the selling and marketing, free of the responsibility of production and the twenty-five staff. And so it proved, sales kept at the same volume and the two converters we used were very efficient and we were making a profit.

I was in my office one morning when Kath rang through. 'There's someone here to see you about transport,' she informed me. 'OK send him in,' and in walks Roger Hunt. Roger Hunt as we all know played for Liverpool and was in the England World Cup winning team of 1966. What's he doing round here asking to see me, he must be lost. But lost he wasn't. He was drumming up business for the family haulage firm of Hunt Bros. I often saw their wagons on the motorway. Surely thinks I, he doesn't want to talk about boring transport, but then he might be fed up to the back teeth talking about boring football. What are we going to talk about then? Please not the weather. It's an interesting observation, here is someone well known still in the 1980s a very good ambassador for the family firm and he's going round hoping to drum up business talking about transport. All the men who he meets only want to talk about football. I wonder how much new business he got. Unfortunately, none from us, we had a very good transport company, and we did touch on football a little. I walked into Kath's office and said, 'That was a surprise.'

'What was?' she asks

'Roger Hunt him calling here.'

'Who'?

'Roger Hunt! He played for England in the 1966 World Cup.'

'Oh.'

'Don't you know him?'

'No.'

Women they never cease to amaze.

Things were so good I got a new car, not just any car but a brand-new car. Not that I'm particularly into cars but at least it demonstrated we could afford one. I decided we needed someone to run the supply and fix side of the ceiling business. The cash sales of the ceilings from the showroom Kath ran. I appointed a guy of around early thirties who had experience in the construction industry and in selling. I could concentrate now fully on the insulation side of the business and business steadily grew on both fronts.

The development and introduction of new products I had always been interested in, introducing these helped you to stay ahead of the game. Glass fibre as everybody knows is not a nice product to handle. Why not encase it in polythene? We did this with the acoustic pads, granted these were made of mineral wool and in slab form but mineral wool is a similar type of material with the same unpleasant characteristics, itchy, dusty, and not nice to handle. If rolls of glass fibre were encased in polythene these irritations would be eliminated, and so we set about experimenting. We found micro-perforated fire-retardant polythene. This would allow the glass fibre to breath. One of our converters made some trial samples and they fulfilled the criteria. We decided on a name 'Insuleeze,' we produced a leaflet. Oh yes did we produce a leaflet.

A representative from an advertising agency called to see me. I explained what we did, showed him our products and extolled the virtues of our new product. This is quite revolutionary making glass fibre pleasant to handle a world first. 'Have you any literature on it?' he asked, 'Oh yes' handing him the leaflet. He perused it, then a disquiet silence. He half spoke. 'Sorry?' I said. 'You have spelled environment wrong, you have missed the n out. 'Emblazoned across the front was ENVIROMENTALY FRIENDLY GLASS FIBRE. My early days back at Jack's offices had come home to roost. No cause for amusement this time. This was costing us money.

We now needed to sell it, after the reprint of the leaflet. We marketed this through a few testing adverts and editorials in the building journals. We started receiving a few enquiries and small orders. These were from architects and individuals in the building industry, mainly for use in their own homes. After six months of nothing spectacular we received a letter from one of the main build journals inviting us or mainly me down to the Savoy in London. The advertisements we had put in their journal had generated sufficient response and enquiries to be included in the annual awards for the newest and most innovative product. So down to the smoke I trots in my best finery. Now only being used to lunch at Geoff's chippy down the street this was a new experience.

I entered the palatial splendour of the Savoy and made first a visit to the gents toilet and there encountered my first new experience. I was met on entering by a man in liveried attire who led me to the urinal (obviously the patrons of this establishment can't find it themselves). Then he stood a few feet behind me, while I relieved myself of four hours of travel. Once zipped up (thank goodness that wasn't in the service) he led me to a sink turned on the tap and again stood a few feet behind me while I washed my hands. I turned off the tap (relieving him of one of his jobs) and he handed me a towel, I dried my hands and left. Should I have offered him a tip? The obvious one would be, don't come in here unless you're desperate. Should I need to go again I'll use the bush, outside. I must see the committee at my local Labour club and suggest they introduce the same service.

I was directed to the appropriate room where the event was happening. There were at least twenty tables with eight placements on each. I found my named station and joined my fellow hopefuls. The man to my right introduced himself. He was from the Forestry Commission and was employed in marketing. 'You're from the head office I presume not from one of the branches?' I enquired. He replied yes without a smile. A fun afternoon this is going to be. He enquired who and where I was from. I satisfied his curiosity with a brief description of our UK and international operations omitting we had a total staff of two.

The eight marketeers on the table, I gleamed from overheard conversation, were from mainly well-known and multinational companies. I could hear strains of marketing budgets and my forestry friend enunciated an insight into his, obviously the postage stamp ours was calculated on did not impress. The top table was made up of senior representatives of the construction industry. They were the judge and jury for the prize on offer. We concluded the meal and convivial conversation, and the formal proceedings began. There were a couple of short speeches proclaiming how well everybody had done, and the usual how impressive and difficult a decision it had been to choose the winners, then the announcement.

There are three prizes, first, second and third, said the speaker, I will start with the third. This is for and he named the product, and it goes to and he named the company. The second is for the product 'Insuleeze' and it goes to Hartnell and Rose Ltd. I de waxed my ears and rose from the chair and made my way to the top table. I shook hands and received the large, engraved trophy. And that is when I caused the embarrassment. I slipped him the £200. As if I would, won on merit and merit alone. I walked back to the table a little dazed viewed by 150 piercing eyes. The guys at the table congratulated me and some shook hands apart from 'forest man'. Whose congratulatory response was 'How come you've won that?' And in my untested principal of victorious magnanimity, 'Because ours is better than yours,' I informed him. And to really twist the knife 'Use a postage stamp when you next work out your marketing budget.' Now it is said first is everything, second is nowhere, tell that to those who haven't won anything, and I haven't got a clue of who came first. And frankly I couldn't give a damn.

Now as the company progressed, we developed a number of successful innovative products, but none won a prize. The one that did was the least successful and to put it more accurately the biggest flop. Why you may ask, I will tell you. I had my doubts from the beginning, and that is not being clever after the event. Number one: We were introducing a product into a market of which we had no experience and one that was completely different from our own. We were in the acoustic insulation market; this was thermal insulation. The term insulation may be the same but that is the only connection. This was a market with very high-volume products. Producing glass fibre rolls encased in polythene was best done at source with the manufacturer. It needed the manufactures stamp on both production and marketing. Number two: The installation of glass fibre in new housing and most other commercial projects was done by specialist companies. Price was the main factor. There were no regulations for glass fibre to be wrapped. Wrapping obviously increased the cost. Contractors or developers would therefore not use or specify a product that was more expensive when there was no regulation demanding it. Because it was nicer and more pleasant to use was not their concern.

And so, the orders came from individuals who were installing it in their own home. This included architects, small builders (below five foot two) and even the head buyer from one of the national house builders for use in his own home not the 20,000 they were building for others. The deliveries were all over the UK in small amounts. It was more a charitable service we were providing, and so we decided to call it a day with this award-winning failure. What was the lesson learned? Stick to what you know and do it well. Oh yes one other thing. If you ever go to the Savoy go to the toilet before you go, and don't drink.

I had a little satisfaction from the escapade. Six months later the largest manufacturer of glass fibre would you believe started producing it wrapped in polythene. Well I never. Had they heard about our product, had they seen our adverts, had they read about the award? You bet they had.

Business was steady but good. Kath proved she was the efficient one-woman band I had always anticipated. Ben with the ceilings was also proving good both with the sales and running the supply and fix jobs. I think I could go on holiday, and so with the family my lads were now nineteen and seventeen we decided to push the boat out and go to New York and Boston, I had relations in Boston. What is this you may ask to do within the context of this book or business? Well indirectly it has, it was through the pursuit of business on our return to the UK that shone a light on misplaced conceptions.

We stayed in New York in the heart of it just of Times Square. Now New York had a reputation for killings, muggings and other tourist attractions. We asked the concierge if it was safe to walk. 'Sure,' he says, 'just stick with the crowds,' and so we did, walking all over. The lads also went out by themselves. They thought they could manage without dad as minder. We never experienced or saw any trouble or problem. When asked, folk were helpful and courteous. The stay in New York, touring around Boston and meeting the relations, made a very enjoyable holiday.

On returning to the UK there were two incidents that occurred within a month of our return that turned on its head my perception of two places. On the first weekend after our return Jack's daughter was getting married. The reception was held in a major hotel in the centre of town. On leaving to collect my car at 11.30pm the concierge asked, 'Can I help you sir?' 'I'm just leaving to pick up my car,' I informed him. 'Oh, that's fine sir, it's just we don't advise anyone to go out in the town on a Saturday night.' New York a few weeks previous the concierge offers 'Just stick with the crowds you'll be fine.' Who would have thought that you'd be safer in New York than my home town, dear old Bolton.

A couple of weeks later I had an appointment in Gloucester. I parked in a side street just off the city centre, I was on the phone (the days when mobiles were like a brick) when there was a tapping on the passenger window. I turned and observed a man who could be best described of Rastafarian appearance, dressed very smart, shirt, tie, suited, with long dreadlocks. He was pointing and gesturing to open the door. I indicated to him I was speaking on the phone. I then heard a tapping on the roof. He was leaning with his right hand on the roof and through the sunroof I could see he was holding an eight-inch bladed knife which he was tapping on the glass, I indicated for him to go away. He brought the knife down to the passenger window and held it for me to see. He then lowered it to the door and scratched a cross into the paint. I cancelled the phone call, offering to the caller I had something else on my mind at the moment. I was mad, should I confront him, but this was tinged with the possible consequences of such an action. He was now gesturing for me to go, and I concluded it was best to do so. I reached for the ignition, but the keys were not in it. I felt in my pockets they were not there. Had I left them in the door? To find out I would have to get out. In this short interval he was getting more aggravated. I jumped out quickly he jumped back obviously not expecting me to have done so. The keys were on the seat I was sat on them. He said, 'Are you a copper? No you're not,' and he held out the knife threateningly, 'Fuck off' he said, 'this is a black area.' I unquestioningly carried out his command.

Who'd have believed New York safer than Bolton and Gloucester, my perception of the three turned on its head. Treat with a slight scepticism what you are led to believe by the press, media, rumour or other sources. First-hand knowledge provides a more realistic perception.

CHAPTER FOURTEEN

Things are Looking up

I met an ex-neighbour whom I hadn't seen for some time I asked how he was and how the family were, he said they were fine but unfortunately his business had collapsed. I expressed my condolences and my surprise as I thought it was doing well. 'It is,' he replied 'the buildings just fallen down. 'Our landlords had mentioned that the gatehouse we occupied may be knocked down. This therefore made it necessary to look for new premises. We were now in a position financially to do so. I didn't want an experience with a similar misunderstanding or possible rumours as my ex-neighbour. We found an abattoir that was being converted into five industrial units, one of them was ideal. There was ample parking at the front. You entered through a front door into a large area which would make an ideal showroom and reception. Two further offices plus a kitchen were off a small corridor, which led through into a warehouse. At the rear was a large communal gated area which could accommodate large wagons.

The new premises were only around twenty years old. This in itself gave an uplift of the spirit and a more confident feeling. They offered a far better impression to visitors than the hundred year old ones we had vacated. Financially we were in a far better position but certainly not yet one where we could sit back and enjoy the fruits of our labours. Kath was pleased to move; she would now occupy a light modern showroom fully deserved for her dedication and loyalty.

I needed another brainstorm and with a heaven-sent bolt of lightning I had one. There was a problem with suspended ceilings the mineral fibre type could absorb sound and the metal type with the pads we produced. This would reduce the noise in the area where the ceiling was installed, but it would not stop it travelling thought the ceiling into other areas. This was a problem in modern office construction, where partitions were installed up to the underside of the suspended ceiling. The sound would travel through the void and conversation in one office could be heard in others. Not good, especially if it was confidential.

The remedy for treating this was to install a curtain in the ceiling void on the lines of the partitions. The foam-lead curtain we supplied addressed this, but it was not suitable in many situations. Glass fibre or mineral wool rolls laid across the back of the ceiling had some effect but made access to the services in the void very difficult. So, what is the answer? A tile made of plasterboard bonded on the one side with the acoustic foam we supplied. The plasterboard produced a barrier the foam placed uppermost in the void would absorb any sound that had penetrated. The foam also with a little overlap of the plasterboard provided a gasket seal around the ceiling grid. It was removed with the tile when access was required. One of our manufacturers could easily produce it. We had it acoustically tested and it proved very effective. We called it Soundblocker it does what it says on the tin. A simple leaflet distributed to all ceiling contractors, and adverts and editorials in the building journals was its entry into the market

We received an enquiry from a northwest local authority for sound insulation in a small office in the Town Hall. This seemed an Ideal contract to install the new product. Normally we would supply only to the contractors. Being the first contract and order it offered the opportunity to test it in site conditions. We decided therefore to install it ourselves. The ceiling fixers completed the job and reported back.

'How did it go?' I asked

'Fine, but they were very hard to fit in the grid,' was their reply.

'They shouldn't have been,' I countered.

'It was the foam that was the problem. It compressed and was tight onto the grid.'

'Which way did you put them in?' I enquired.

' We put them in with the foam downward onto the back of the ceiling tile.'

'You've put them in the wrong way, the foam should be uppermost.'

And there they are as far as I'm aware to this day, obviously still doing a good job.

This product has proved successful over nearly thirty years with sales of many thousands of square metres. As far as I am aware the only ones that have been installed incorrectly were by yours truly. And what do you learn from this? If you want a job doing, get someone else to do it.

As I have previously mentioned I have always had a good relationship with the ceiling contractors, having received through them many contracts which have proved instrumental in forming my career. Treat them fairly, honestly and with support and you will be duly rewarded, and one such lead was now to set the new product on its way. A contractor had received an enquiry for the ceiling in the new baggage handling hall of a major regional airport. The ceiling required good sound insulation to stop the noise from the baggage handling services in the ceiling void penetrating into the hall below. He had received our information and thought the new product could possibly be suitable for the contract, and so it proved. Of course, it wasn't quite so straight forward, but after meetings and samples and mock-ups and tests, the order came through. This was a large, prestigious job and I would certainly have to make sure the panels were installed the right way up, and they were, and they were successful. So, when you are waiting for your luggage at a carousel and there's not a sound coming through the ceiling, you are obviously in the right airport.

CHAPTER FIFTEEN

Money Matters

The term cash is king is very true. The majority of business is run on credit, usually allowing a month for invoices to be settled. The consequence of this can be slow payment or even no payment. The building industry is a prime example of this. The main contractors often have the subcontractor dangling on a string. If there is any excuse for delayed payment or withholding retention monies, they often will take advantage of it causing subcontractors to go bust because of this.

We as a manufacturer were not directly affected as all our business was with subcontractors or the end user, we were though indirectly affected. If a subcontractor was delayed in being paid, they could delay payment to us or use it as an excuse. Thankfully the majority paid within reasonable time but where they did not you had to assess the situation and implement legal action if needed.

One action that is very effective but seldom used is a garnishee. This is obtained through the court and it is served on the third party that is a company who owes money to the company who owes you. The difficulty is finding a company who is a debtor to your debtor, and the amount they owe needs to be greater than what is owed to you. You serve the garnishee on them and they are legally obliged to pay you the amount owed by your debtor.

We served this action successfully twice on two separate companies. On both occasions on finding the company to serve it on we had a little luck. The first one I was informed by a customer of ours whose wife was over the accounts of a company who owed our debtor. I obtained a garnishee via the court and took the paperwork to the third party. I saw the company secretary he accepted it and they paid us. The second one was a little more involved.

Our debtor was a subcontractor who worked for main contractors or direct for an end user. I needed to find who he was currently carrying out work for. The easiest way was to follow him to a contract. I arrived therefore at his premises very early in the morning before he arrived. I parked a hundred metres away and waited. He arrived shortly after, went inside and came back out within ten minutes, got back into his car and drove off, and so did I in hot pursuit. The police when tailing a car often use two vehicles and it's obvious why. To follow a vehicle while trying not to be detected by your quarry is not easy. You need to stay at least two cars behind and the longer the journey goes on the harder it becomes. They may have managed it in Hollywood, but they never filmed in Blackburn.

Jumping the occasional traffic light to stay in pursuit is unavoidable. To stop more cars coming between from side streets or roundabouts is impossible. And then as if a starting gun had been fired, we were off, well my debtor friend was. I'd been clocked. A sudden left turn up a back street which he obviously hoped I would miss or if I didn't it would confirm my pursuit, and I confirmed it. Back street, side street, cobbled street, right turns, left turns, short street, long street, Monaco Grand Prix was not in the same class, there you don't speed down back streets nor avoid wheelie bins. Lost him damn it, this man obviously did this for a hobby back to the drawing board.

This company also did joinery and building work for main contractors. A good friend of mine was the company accountant for a large northwest contractor, could it be he did subcontract work for them? A bit of a long shot but nothing lost, I can ask. So, I phoned my mate and explained the situation. He instantly recognised the name of the company, and after checking confirmed they owed them more than their debt to us. Can

I serve you therefore with a garnishee I requested, and I'll buy you a pint? Yes, go ahead he said, in that case I'll make it two. I would have loved to have seen the reaction of both of these incumbents when they received settlement of their account less the monies that had been paid to us.

Throughout my personal life I have never owed money other than a mortgage or personal loans. I have paid my bills or monies owing on time especially to individuals. This applied also to business. We paid even when business was tight and believe you me at times it was tight. I have never liked owing money. Unfortunately, this does not apply to some individuals where owing money does not faze them. They will deliberately or with certain indifference play the game with other people's finances or indeed lives. I have no time for them. I can understand when the legal process can be costly, slow, and deliberately manipulated to avoid payment, that more direct action may be considered.

I reluctantly admit I have only ever once partly engaged in it. We were owed money by a small building contractor for a ceiling job we had done. He had promised to pay on numerous occasions but never came up with the goods, I lost patience. I called at a job where he was working, he came out and we stood by my car. I guided him to the boot and opened it there in it lay a baseball bat, which I had bought for my lads on our trip to the US.

'I don't play the game myself,' I informed him, 'but I know someone who does. Have the money on my desk tomorrow morning' and he did.

This piece of threatened thuggery was suggested by a colleague who had used it with similar success. May I say I didn't know anyone who played the game nor would I have tried to find one, but my builder friend didn't know that, this is the one and only time I ever engaged in such a practice. I have lost a number of so-called business friends by pursuing legal action against them. I have also avoided taking legal action against certain companies or individuals knowing them or the financial circumstance which they have found themselves in and indeed have been thanked for not doing so. It is a decision in business you have got to take without sentiment. For you also need to survive.

In November 1999 the Nuffield Foundation commissioned and published a report on the general public's attitude and opinions of Judges and the judiciary. It was at the time the largest survey of its kind ever conducted. It found that only 53% thought they would get a fair hearing and two out of three thought Judges were out of touch with the ordinary people. This was well publicised in the news at the time and by coincidence within a week of its publication I had reason to concur with its findings. We had instituted legal proceedings against a company to obtain the money they owed to us. The proceedings necessitated me attending a hearing to appeal the case before a judge in his chambers in Leeds. Our solicitor had advised I attend on my own as the case was reasonably straightforward. This would save us considerable money by avoiding him having to travel to Leeds. Little did I know the judge, would personify in every detail the findings of the Nuffield report.

On entering his chambers, he gestured slightly off hand for me to sit down. He was around mid-sixties in age. He wore the conventional uniform of immaculate pinstripe suit and fountain pen.

'Are you represented?' he asked in a stern no nonsense antithesis of a Yorkshire accent.

'No,' I replied.

'That would not have happened years ago,' presumably referring to the Dickensian era. 'You do realise you will struggle getting this money?' said in a curt offhand manner.

Who is this guy? I had come here to hopefully receive his assistance in obtaining our debt. The debtor had not even turned up, yet I was feeling the guilty one. He scanned the papers before him and uttered a few more offhand comments.

'I find in your favour' delivered in a magnanimous tone and a nod of the head indicating you may leave.

Even though he had found in our favour his dismissive, demeaning attitude annoyed me, I felt if the debtor had come and had been represented, he may have looked on him with more favour. He offered no perception or appreciation of the cost of being represented for a full day, when the case certainly did not necessitate it. I certainly did not expect or anticipate sympathy, perhaps a little understanding and certainly a more civil attitude. I have known two judges socially, both very friendly, good company and with a good sense of humour. When you have suffered with a frustrated vocation of wishfully dispensing sentences of three years hard labour or sending a boat full of felons to Australia, and instead you end up administering justice on a two-bit bad debt court in Leeds, it obviously manifests itself in the manner or demeanour of my learned Judge.

I reported back the outcome to our solicitor and explained I feel like sending him a letter indicating my displeasure at his attitude. Why don't you he said and let me have a look at it before you send it so this I did, and he advised a very slight alteration keeping 95%of my script including a reference to the Nuffield report. I posted it to the judge addressed to Leeds Crown Court and I got a reply.

With reference to your letter of the 30th Nov, if you wish to take this matter further consult a solicitor.

He may have been a dispenser of justice, but his main concern was keeping the legal profession in the financial status to which they had become accustomed. In case you are wondering, we did get the money.

Do you know who you really are? How you would react in an unknown situation or circumstance. Are you a hero or a coward? Have you ever been tried and tested to find out? I may have an inkling I was a good runner in my younger days. Do you know what untested dark traits lie beneath? Would some circumstances change or alter you. You go through life on the whole not really being tested. I think generally throughout my working life I have had a reasonably easy-going persona. My easy-going persona was tried and tested in the period when we were in the mill. I found myself in a position I certainly hadn't planned for and one that was alien to me. I had to learn and learn quickly. It brought home a reality of life, a hardening of attitude and less tolerance. The experience brought out a more aggressive or assertive nature one that expressed itself in the threatening of our debtor with a baseball bat. I am sure I would never have contemplated such action prior to my experience in the mill. Was there lying dormant a more aggressive and more worrying a violent nature, that the circumstances and experience brought to the surface? I got no pleasure by taking the action I did and never indulged in it or any of a similar nature again, pursuing thereafter a legal formula to obtain bad debts.

Did I have any conscience or regrets about taking the action with our debtor with the baseball bat, no I didn't. But I might have had if I hadn't obtained the money.

CHAPTER SIXTEEN

Things are Realy Looking up

We were doing steady business on all fronts. We now had three named products, Soundblocker, Soundstop, and Coustifoam. The ceilings were also bringing in a steady income. Jack's middle son Julian who was in his mid-twenties and had been living abroad was coming back to the UK. He suggested he thought he would be an asset to the company. He had a degree in physics and had studied acoustics. He would bring technical expertise to the company and computer skills. A younger person, he would bring us into the modern world, and so he joined us, and Jack's suggestion proved right. We could now start manufacturing again.

Mark my youngest son had left university and was deciding his future. He joined us with a friend Dave to do the manufacturing. We bought a spray booth, a large flatbed saw for cutting the foam and plasterboard, plus a stacker truck. We also needed industrial racking for storage. Now industrial racking and domestic differences mixed together can be lethal, not obvious ingredients to produce a near-death experience. I found a company who was selling some and arranged a meeting at their premises. The boss introduced himself and said the racking was at his house five miles away and we would go in his car. We eventually come into open country on a long straight narrow road. Coming towards us some distance off was another car. Our speed was moderately fast and so appeared to be the other vehicles neither slowing down. The two drivers seemed to be engaged in the game of Chicken and I was not keen to be the wishbone. I was considering grabbing the wheel when suddenly my chauffeur decided life was worth living and swung sharply to the left onto the grass verge and careered along it without any reduction in speed while the other car passed us. 'That's the bloody wife,' my driver informs me. 'We had an argument this morning. I bought the racking on the condition they delivered it. He informed me they were selling up and moving to a house on a road. I hoped it was a wide one.

We were up and running, well walking. Within a short period of time, we received an order for the internal acoustic lining for the new Glasgow exhibition and conference centre. This is the armadillo-shaped building on the Clyde. Mark and Dave were performing well and were joined by another of their friends Sid. We had a happy little workforce all mates and very capable. What a difference from the previous incumbents. The order went well it was a good start and for a very prominent and prestigious building.

In the pursuit of business travelling and driving are a fundamental part. I had done this for years. One of the consequences of doing so, are punctures. The imperative of keeping appointments hones a skill at changing a wheel matched only by a Formula One pit stop, but not this day. I was returning from Yorkshire on the M62, I had reached the highest point 1220 feet (372m), indeed the highest point of any motorway in the country. It was raining horizontal backed by the usual hurricane, often found around these quarters, and lo and behold I had one a puncture that is. I pulled onto the hard shoulder. The culprit was the back offside wheel flat as the proverbial fluke. I got out the necessary cutlery. The wind and rain were off the scale. I placed the jack in the appropriate housing. Being on the outside of the hard shoulder my back was four feet away from the passing juggernauts and the occasional cyclist. The spray generated by these would have filled Windermere in a couple of minutes. Sod this for a bunch of fairies thinks I, so I promptly got in the car reversed up the banking and back onto the hard shoulder facing the other way, the wrong way. I was now on the inside. It was almost tropical. I change the wheel put the punctured one in the boot and slammed it. Oh dear! I had dropped the keys in the boot while lifting the wheel out and the only way to open this was by the key, no release handle. What design guru thought that one up. It was 4.30pm on a Friday, I was soaked and miles from anywhere. Why doesn't somebody invent a phone where you can phone from anywhere.

I walked to the nearest emergency phone, the operator informed me the nearest Ford agent where you may get a key was in Rochdale three weeks walk away. I returned to the car, this was a saloon the only way into the boot was via the back of the back seat. Like a man possessed I put my hands on the top and pulled. There were twangs and bangs and cracks and thuds. I pulled the back down as low as possible, but it would not lie flat. The opening into the boot was small this was further reduced by two cross members. The angle of the back of the seat was about twenty-five degrees which I had to manoeuvre myself over. The opening would allow my head and one shoulder through. I could see the keys at the far side of the boot, but could I reach them? I squeezed through the cross member with my arm fully outstretched.

I was now in a position slightly stuck, with my head just in the boot and my feet out of the door, in a car facing the wrong way on the hard shoulder. Surely a police car must come past, and what would he be met with. The car facing the wrong way, the back door open, a pair of feet sticking out and half the body in the boot. The police must witness many strange situations, but I'd bet this would be a first. Police not a sign, keys yes and in my hand. I reversed up the bank and re-joined the direction from whence I came, wet but happy. As for Formula One pit stops, they are a piece of cake.

The next day I bought an emergency puncture spray the one that inflates your tyre with foam. By coincidence one of my Christmas presents that year was a magnetic spare key box that was fitted under the wheel arch or some other suitable hiding place, better late than never.

Back to important matters. When we first developed Soundblocker and before we had introduced it to the market, I showed it to an ex-MD of one of the metal ceiling manufactures and a ceiling contractor whom I both knew. I was interested in their opinion and any suggestions they may have. They both thought it seemed a good product addressing an acknowledged problem and wished it well. Their endorsement was assuring, my mistake was I never got them to sign a confidentiality agreement, indeed I never thought of it. The consequence of which stopped us possibly obtaining a patent on it. I had shown and disclosed the product which meant should they copy or produce it or simply disclose to someone else the idea for it, the original idea and whose it was could be challenged and disputed. The patent attorney who we consulted knowing this, advised not to proceed with a full patent application, but just go along with a 'patent applied for' which would last for a considerable time and give some protection within this period. This was a hard lesson to learn but all in the untutored education of experience.

Soundblocker had been very well received, so much so we had an enquiry from the largest ceiling tile manufacturers in the world. Could we supply them with Soundblockers? They would market them under a different name, and would supply them where the contract demanded, with their ceiling tiles. This looked a very promising prospect. The outcome was, we received steady orders direct from them but never in any great amount. The contractors often knew or presumed we were the manufacturers and although it was a named product that was specified, they would order from us, as our price may have been lower. We had offered them a price so they could match ours when selling, if they chose not to do so that was their decision. We therefore received orders which unknowingly were their specification. Being also specialist manufacturers of sound stopping products carried a certain weight, but we were minnows compared to their size, dominance and reputation in the ceiling industry. But here's the key. If you can specialise in a certain market i.e., acoustics, you can hold your own against much bigger companies who cannot offer the speciality you possess. O yes I forgot, also if your price is lower it helps.

When Julian joined us, he brought us into the twentieth century. Computers, good heavens, we now had them we could get rid of the abacus. His degree in physics/acoustics gave us a greater technical ability and confidence. We could now do acoustic test well with the right equipment, far better than our previous tests, where I stood at one side of a wall shouting, 'Can you hear me mother?' Mark and Dave had done an excellent job starting up the manufacturing, but they had decided to move on.

Alex who Mark knew joined us, he had just left university and was waiting to go to teacher training college. He's still waiting, but his current position of Managing Director of the company might be an obstacle. He acquired a qualification in acoustics, and as they say the rest is history. Well not yet there is a bit more to tell.

Now with Julian and Kath, whose loyalty was built into the foundation stone of the company, and whose ability and experience with customers was second to none, we had a very good management team. I could now go out more and sell, battles are won from the trenches and that is where I liked to be, but before that I must renew my previously documented philosophy of 'pleasure before business' I may say an experience quite unintentional, but they often proved the best. I had an early morning appointment in Middlesbrough, I had concluded this by the late morning and decided, as it was a nice day, to take the long way back through the Yorkshire dales. Now this is a beautiful part of the country and being a true Lancastrian, it is not easy to acknowledge there's something good that comes from Yorkshire, sad boy. I'd have to drive through it with my eyes partly closed. I may also add I would normally have taken advantage of the rest of the day to call on a couple of contractors, but you have got to have a day off sometime, well half a day. I proceeded through the town of Richmond and then Leyburn onto Wensley and the entrance to Wensleydale. I felt a pang of hunger and a nice pint would also go down well, low and behold that looks a nice pub, and so it was.

I went to the bar and was greeted by a friendly landlord, he served me a pint and I leant against the bar in my well-rehearsed posture. There were three men stood at the bar amiably chatting and three others all sat on separate tables I joined in the conversation with the three. They were on their way to Ripon Races and were leaving shortly, so much for their best laid plans. The minutes ticked by and after half an hour we were still talking. When one of the guys who was sat at a table, got up went over to the piano (what pub has them now?) and hit the keys with a ragtime version of 'Steamboat Bill.' Now those of tender years may wonder what a ragtime version of Steamboat Bill is. Just take it from me it is good and lively especially when rendered by this guy who knew how to tinkle the ivories. He continued with upbeat sing along songs which we embraced with our slightly lubricated larynx. He played for around twenty minutes and returned to his seat with accompanying applause.

He had certainly livened the ambience if not to party mood certainly to a lifting of the spirit. We continued in conversation for some time when a guy on one of the other tables brought out a penny whistle or a very small flute and struck up 'Phil the Fluter's Ball.' We all knew the tune if not all the words, that was no obstacle to us all joining in and making our own contribution to the said lyrics with the odd little jig thrown in. He continued with a few more well-known Irish ditties which we duly embraced with appropriate jocularity, and then the artist on the third table not to be left out produced paper and comb and accompanied our flutist as would an obvious well practiced virtuoso. This was a weekday afternoon, what was this place like on a Saturday night? To say the ambience was lively and jovial would be an understatement, but we hadn't finished unbeknown it was only the interval, with the star act to come. The artist joined in the bonhomie which they had created, not realising they were only the support acts.

She first appeared at the door; what was Marlene Dietrich, with the familiar hair style, dress and lipstick doing in North Yorkshire especially considering she had been dead for a number of years. She slowly seductively glided to the table of our piano player, lifted her foot onto a chair raised her skirt to above her knee, exposing a garter and looked longingly into the eyes of Mr Piano and in a deep seductive voice sang, 'Falling in love again never wanted to what am I to do, I can't help it.' She glided around the other tables re-enacting, the garter revealing, bewitching the appreciative musicians, while singing all the remaining verses. She returned to the spell bound Mr Piano stroked his cheek and slowly walked out giving a little backward wave. How often the landlady did this I don't know, but presumably this was not for the first time. I have never been in any pub or indeed any establishment where such unexpected, unscripted, spontaneous entertainment was on hand. One of the most memorable afternoons I have ever spent in a drinking establishment, and there have been a few.

I left reluctantly, offering my thanks to the landlord, and unfortunately never saw Marlene again perhaps having done the matinee she was getting ready for the evening performance. My three bar companions never made the races and I have never been back. I met some years later a man who lived in Leyburn the nearest small town, I recalled the afternoon to him he knew the pub and the innkeepers. He confirmed what an excellent pub it was and what great characters they were. Their likes were from a different era, mores the pity.

No business could succeed on my stated philosophy of pleasure before business. I have mentioned it of course to give the narrative a little humour. The meeting I had in Middlesbrough was in the morning probably around 10amand concluded approximately 11.30am, I calculate this by the time I stopped for my quick bite to eat, I would have left home around 7am. Leaving at that time and the meeting lasting one and a half hours, it must have been important. Not to make other calls while in the area would possibly indicate it was successful. I would probably have made others to compensate if it had not been so. The meeting I had was with who? and what about, was it successful or a failure? I haven't got a clue, not a jot of remembrance, unlike the afternoon.

I have met a number of very successful men in my career and on the whole they have been what you would describe as decent, indeed quite ordinary guys, unaffected at least outwardly by wealth and success. There are, of course the other type, one such, I first became aware of when I was twelve. He was in his early thirties and although I never spoke to him, I was conscious of his slight arrogance and smartarse demeanour. He was a business associate of the father of a friend of mine which ultimately ended in a fall out between them. His wife had a woman's dress shop lower down the road on which we lived, which my mother frequented. He opened up in the fifties, a car dealership and new showroom in a very prominent position on a main road of the town, which was very successful along I would presume with other businesses.

Other than when I was first aware of him through my friend's father I had only since been twice in his company the first time very briefly in my duplicator repair days when I called to administer the required repair to their machine. He happened to come into the office and confirmed my original opinion of him. He was one of the very few people I did not like. He was the type of guy you would have got great pleasure in the expression of 'getting one over on him' or showing him up. Move on twenty five years and we lived not close but within the same area he in a much bigger house than mine of course. Very occasionally I would see him by sight and then one day I called in my local and who should be the only other person in the pub sat at the bar than Mr Smartarse, I deposited myself on the stool on the side bar. By this time he was well retired and at least twenty years older than me. To him I was a total stranger not having the slightest clue as to who I was.

We sat in silence for a couple of minutes then I thought I'll commence the conversation.

'You used to live on Freshfield Road in the fifties didn't you?' He looked at me but with no acknowledgement but a slightly puzzled expression. 'Your wife had a dress shop on it, and she was blonde' (which she was also attractive, well to a twelve-year-old). Still no response but with the slight puzzled or wary expression, he continued looking at me. Allowing a few seconds pause, I reminded him he had opened Fairfield Motors in the late fifties, he offered a slight nod but no rhetoric. And now for the coup de grace, 'You went into business with Frank Leatham in 1956 and I think you had a bust up with him.' That had the desired effect, but still no verbal response other than 'I'm off' which he conveyed to the landlord, downed what was left of his pint and exited stage left. I got a lot of pleasure in 'getting one over on him' I think that would be the appropriate expression, obviously he did not. Why he did not answer or question me I do not know, I think shock, who the hell was I? and what else may I reveal possibly unnerved him. I never saw him in the pub again. The landlord who was equally surprised did ask me 'How did you know all that?' and I told him with the true and very simple innocent answer. Obviously as was my intention my fellow drinker thought it may somehow have been a little deeper, and my pint did taste a little sweeter.

CHAPTER SEVENTEEN

Geordie Land

Through my extensive travels throughout the UK one of my favourite cities to visit was Newcastle. I had good relations with the contractors and had received valued support from them. My sons where at local universities, Michael at Newcastle and Mark at nearby Sunderland, so my visits were often a mixture of business and pleasure. The northeast has a very strong identity and that certainly is emphasised in the accent and dialect.

In the days before satellite navigation there were only two ways to find a direction to a street or road. One was the indispensable A-Z maps the other was to ask someone. In all the years of my extensive driving and through the experience acquired of asking strangers directions, there are three persons you should avoid asking. One, a woman, if she knew the street or road she could not explain how to get there. Two, an Argentinean they wouldn't even have heard of the street or road. Three a Geordie, he may know the street or road like the back of his hand, but you wouldn't be able to understand a word he said. I have travelled the length and breadth of the UK speaking to people with strong local accents or dialects including heavy Glaswegian. I have spoken to many foreigners in the UK and abroad with strong broken English. The only place, in all the world when someone is supposedly speaking English and when I couldn't understand one word was in Newcastle and that was asking a man directions. The only British documentary I have watched on television which had subtitles when they were interviewing people was on Newcastle. So if you ever visit that fair city and you need directions make sure you either have a sat nav an A-Z map, or a translator.

Luckily with my business connections I didn't need a translator just a sharp pencil and preferably a knowledge of football. No other area in the country with the possible exception of Liverpool would the beautiful game be a near necessity in conversation. I have called on contractors to be met with 'I see Bolton lost on Saturday,' and this is when the Wanderers where in the third division. The embarrassment was I sometime didn't know if they had, but to admit to this might put a dent in our relationship. 'Yes, they're struggling at the moment,' I'd offer, for goodness sake don't ask me my thoughts on the match. I would have felt more comfortable admitting I was the Yorkshire Ripper (he was still being sought). I have often wished Newcastle would have achieved more for the sake of their supporters and for the benefit of English football.

Business was my first priority but pleasure always ran a close second. One such memorable night possibly cost me an order. I emphasise possibly, no proof has been found to confirm definitely. A friend of Michael's at university was celebrating his twenty-first and as I was in the area I was invited. Now I ask you what sensible late forty-year-old would not wish to go on a piss up with twenty-one-year-old university students? The sobering restraint on a potentially overindulgent night was that the celebrant's parents were also to attend. At eight o clock the following morning that theory had gone for a Burton. I had an appointment at 9.30am with the North East Health Authority. Luckily my hotel was in reasonable walking distance of their offices and this I took advantage of affording me quick walking and deep breathing. I arrived outside the building with ten minutes to spare. I continued this hopefully sobering action by walking backward and forward along the pavement. To anyone observing this pacing it would have appeared unusual if not a little suspicious. I trusted my potential order provider was not an observer.

When feeling as best described as a little under the weather you can overreact, to compensate for the demeanour your condition would naturally portray. I took a deep breath put on my sunny side spring is here expression and entered the building. The receptionist directed me to the office of my appointee. I knock and entered at his command. It was a large office and the first thing I saw was a chaise lounge that could be handy in case I need to lie down. This was the only time in my career where I have conducted business with the debilitating consequences of a hangover and surprisingly it is not conducive with a successful outcome. My request to conduct the meeting by my initial thought from the more comforting position of lying on the chaise lounge made for an abrupt termination of proceedings. I have reminded Rupert when we have met over the years he still owes me £20,000 in compensation for a lost order and the dearest night out I've ever had.

As I have previously described the extent of business miles travelled brought circumstances that those who drive more conventional mileage would possibly not experience. Two such instances occurred on two trips to the northeast. I had concluded my business in Newcastle and was continuing my journey to Dundee. My journey took me over the Forth Road Bridge. On reaching mid-span the traffic stopped and I joined the queue. For a number of seconds there was no obvious difference than stopping in any situation then it clicked in. You could not stop moving, up down left right involuntary movements, gripping the steering wheel had no effect to reduce it. You were experiencing the natural movements of the bridge and believe me it moved. What an experience it could be in high winds. I opened the window to be met with a cacophony of sound, banging squeaking grating the stresses and strains of the steel. I could view the water many feet below through the gap between the carriageways. This along with the movement and noise heightened your awareness of your vulnerability should the highly unlikely unthinkable happen. Driving across it you obviously have no sensation of this. If you are thinking of doing so don't be put off it's been there for many years and will be for many more.

The oil embargo of 1973–74 caused by the Arab–Israeli war resulting in the short supply of petrol was not conducive to anyone who depended on its ready supply in furthering their career the queues at petrol stations were a new experience. Stealing petrol from car tanks by inserting a rubber tube and the necessary sucking to activate the flow was cultivating petrol junkies. I had thankfully not been subject to this unsavoury activity, only to succumb to it even with my acquiescence some years after the conflict was over. I was returning from a trip to Newcastle down the M6 when the fuel gauge indicating near zero necessitated I put a little fuel in the tank. Thankfully a service station the one with the large tower not that I would mention its name was close at hand. I took the slip road and drove to the petrol pump. I filled the tank to the maximum and went to the kiosk to pay and presented my well used major credit card beginning with the letter 'B.'

'I'm afraid we don't accept this card sir the cashier,' informed me, 'in which case you'll have to pay cash.'

'I don't have sufficient cash on me,' I inform her.

'In that case we will have to take the petrol back,' she informs me.

And so an attendant arrived with rubber tube and a number of receptacles. He inserted the said tube into the tank and sucked, kindly leaving an estimated amount in the tank to get me home.

Very surprising even then that a service station on a major motorway did not accept the most popular credit card in the market, but rest assured they do now.

CHAPTER EIGHTEEN

Above and Below

The company's products and overall market involvement was quite narrow, our mark was the acoustics associated with the suspended ceiling industry. There are two other surfaces in a building, walls and floors. The sound insulation market that these areas commanded was larger than our limited one. We quite often received enquiries for sound insulation to both floors and walls we would pass these to two companies who specialised in these fields. For this we received just a thanks, no monetary reward, and you cannot live on thanks alone, something must be done.

Walls were the first to receive our attention. To stop or reduce the transmission of sound you need mass. Half a metre of concrete is effective but not very practical. The criteria demanded. A product with a minimum thickness while, providing the maximum performance. We produced a composite panel of three elements which matched the criterion. It has taken four lines to describe this. The design testing and manufacture took relatively longer, but we were now able to offer a walling sound insulating product. Our once friendly recipient of our generous leads was no longer too friendly, when we informed him, he had new competition. Maxiboard was the name and with the press release, adverts and circulars we were now in the game. Slowly but surely the enquiries came, we were getting there with products for all seasons, well nearly all.

Our main market was the commercial and industrial sector. We did receive calls from the general public the problem was always next door, noise coming through party walls into the lounge or bedrooms. You took them with caution, although in some cases you satisfied their demands, in others you didn't. They still may be able to hear the sound albeit reduced. If the source was a deaf neighbour with TV on full blast, an aspiring drummer or rock group, you may have a problem. With commercial contracts there may be an acoustician involved or you knew the insulation performance required, and these could be tested to see you met them. No such parameter or testing was available or necessary for private enquiries on domestic property. Should the client not be satisfied you then may not get paid. You had to pick and be very careful what jobs you chose to do. I had a phone call from a man who asked.

'I'm ringing to see if you can help me you do acoustics, don't you?'

'Yes,' I volunteered

'I've got music coming from next door.'

'What is it the radio or what?' I asked.

'A brass band,' he replied. 'They've started using it as a practice room can you give me some advice?'

'Not an easy thing to stop. I think the best advice I can give, is to make sure they play something you like.'

Luckily, he saw the funny side. I advised he saw the council; I didn't want the challenge.

That enquiry was extreme. A slightly lesser one was an enquiry we received from a fire station to insulate the control room from external noise. This was a conventional job, and we fulfilled their demands. On leaving after completion, I was talking to one of the senior officers, he informed me he'd joined at the age of twenty had worked hard and had just climbed the ladder to get to his current position, said without a smile or recognition that he'd missed his true vocation. This has no relevance to the job, acoustics or any other connection associated with the business, it was just an amusing comment reinforced more so being unintentional.

There are only two gears in business, forward and back. We were moving forward very nicely and had no intention of engaging reverse. Our only absent product was for floors, we probably received more enquiries for these than for the walls. Enquiries for these were also passed to another company, one of a number of companies producing acoustic flooring. All the products were based on a solid board, chipboard or similar bonded to other material forming a laminate. They were all rigid producing a conventional floor and were mainly installed in flats and apartments both in new build and refurbished.

In business you can produce products and services the same as others i.e., your competition or you can be different. If you are producing the same as others, to succeed you have got to be equally as good and ideally better, or cheaper. If you produce a different product you have got to be equally as good, but it is not as imperative to be cheaper. There are many facets to these scenarios but in principle they're true. We as in our other products preferred to be different. With products that are the same or similar the principle is tried and tested. With one that is different you have got to establish it. The difference made will hopefully offer advantages, but it must perform its main function, in this case reducing sound transmission.

Julian came up with an Idea for a product that as far as we were aware was the first of its type in the world. We did not broadcast this fact just in case there was some guy in his tropical shed in some speck of a Pacific Island, had done the same. What was it? An acoustic underlay, a product that could be laid onto a conventional floor and a carpet laid on top. It offered all the qualities of a good underlay but in addition sound insulation for both airborne and impact noise. It was constructed of foam sandwiched between two layers of the polymeric barrier we used on the Maxiboard. It was only 1.5cm thick, flexible and could be cut with a knife. Anyone who had an acoustic problem through the floor could take up their existing underlay and replace it with this. Simple end of story and with that I'll finish. Don't think you're getting off so lightly. Its performance figures were good, it was unique it addressed problems other products didn't. Bingo. We named it Acoustilay.

The majority of households are not affected by intrusive external noise from adjoining properties. As a personal appraisal do you suffer from it, do you know anyone who does? Have you heard of anyone affected by it? People go on with their everyday lives never experiencing the problem unaware how many people are victims of unwanted noise. When multi storey apartments and flats are designed from new or as conversions, soundproofing is an integral part of the design. It should conform for walls and floors to British Standards. In a new build the soundproofing would be built into the floor. For conversions of existing buildings, they may wish to keep the existing floor and a soundproofing layer would be placed on top. This would normally be in the form of composite rigid boarding of around 5cm in thickness. This could affect the depth of the skirting board and being a solid board, it would have to be sawn and shaped as necessary.

Acoustically came in 120x120cm flexible mats. It was 1.5cm thick and could be cut with a Stanley Knife, and was simply laid onto the existing floor as an underlay would be. It was therefore ideally suited for remedial contracts. Offering quick installation and at 1.5cm thick had the minimum effect on any increase in floor height. Now how much do you want?

New build and refurbished apartments and flats would often have an acoustician as a consultant in the initial design. Once the contract was completed acoustic tests would be conducted to confirm it conformed to the required standard. Hopefully with this achieved, the occupants could enjoy a peaceful coexistence. In many contracts they did so, unfortunately in others they did not. Problems could occur through the whole of the building. In others it could be in isolated individual apartments. The problem often arose not through a design fault, but through the builder failing to carry out the build as laid out in the specification and design. This may not be a deliberate action to cut cost or time but a mistake by installing an item wrongly or an omission by not installing one at all. This failure would then only be found after occupation.

The consequence of this could mean considerable work and disruption to find the fault and to correct it. It could mean the floors walls or ceilings or part of them being removed. There are two types of noise, annoying and even more annoying, to be more precise, airborne and impact. Airborne is that which travels through the air, radio, television, music, electric drills, etc. Impact is caused by physical connection, footfalls on the floor, knocking on a wall, hammering. The one that is the most prevalent for impact noise is footfalls from the floor above. This was an increasing problem when laminated flooring became the fashion. This in many situations replaced carpet and underlay which both are a good insulator for impact noise, the consequence of which was felt by the people below.

Laminated floors are often now banned in multi-occupied buildings, or permission has got to be given for them to be installed, combined with the appropriate insulation.

If you think paying big money for a flat or apartment would give greater assurance for a peaceful abode, think again. We were invited to stay with friends who had moved to the south coast. They took us on a trip showing us their new environs this included a new development of million pound plus apartments, all with private moorings. This was the late 1990s probably two million plus now. We had a pleasant few days with them. Two weeks later I received a phone call. The caller explained he was the spokesman for the residents in a residential apartment development. They were having sound problems between the apartments and could I send him details of our products. Certainly, give me your address, you've guessed it. The two million pounds with built in surround sound apartments. I resisted offering the advice I gave to the man who lived next to the brass band practice room.

Actions speak louder than words. Well, they do when the recipient has had the phone slammed down in their ear. The recipient was a high-flying London businesswoman. She had a sound problem from the apartment above. Whoever was the culprit I'm surprised she hadn't devoured them alive. She briefly explained her problem, obviously time was the essence. I interceded with a question which she either dismissed or answered very curtly. This continued for a couple of minutes in which she countered or did not seem to hear my advice, but she did hear the slamming down of my phone.

Jill was her name, from our first conversation I never realised we would get so intimate, well first name terms. From my action of gently putting the phone down on her she rang back virtually immediately with a more conciliatory and apologetic tone. She was probably well practiced in having phone calls abruptly terminated. First impressions are generally correct, and I did not like her. I've experienced much practice of that statement in my career. If you dislike someone you may ignore them, have to tolerate them, and keep your contact to the minimum. I have only experienced two people where that statement has been turned on its head. One of them was Jill. Over the next few weeks we chatted, laughed, discussed her sound problem, I sent her samples, concluding in her decision to install Acoustilay in the apartment above. She paid for the occupants to have an overnight stay while this was installed by a company she had organised, a very capable lady. The job was a success. She suggested when I was next in London we should meet and have a coffee or indeed something stronger. We never did.

Acoustilay proved very successful and its success provided an additional bonus in an unforeseen way. Our business up to the introduction of Acoustilay had been mainly with the ceiling industry. We sold the products through distributors or direct to the ceiling contractors. The majority of these had accounts with us. Acoustically was specified by an architect or developer and sold to the flooring Industry, ordered and installed mainly by flooring contractors or carpet installers. None of these had accounts with us. They therefore had to pay by pro forma. Some objected to this but generally they accepted it as this being a new product and one they knew they would not use on a regular bases. The influx of money was a great benefit to our cash flow.

I have previously mentioned how main contractors sometimes withheld retention monies at any opportunity from subcontractors. One particular Acoustilay contract gave me a little satisfaction in reversing this practice. A flooring contractor refused to pay pro forma and said he would contact the main contractor and ask them to place the order. This was one of the top three main contractors in the country who had a reputation for the practice of withholding monies. They telephoned and said they would place the order. I confirmed that would be satisfactory but they had no account with us and they would have to pay pro forma. They refused to do this. After a slight consideration they obviously realised the consequence of changing the specification to another product would require the architect's approval and in addition it would make them responsible should anything go wrong. We received the order and the payment.

This proved without doubt the validity of a quotation by Joe Gormley (ex-president of the National Union of Mineworkers), 'When you've got them buy the balls, their hearts and minds follow.'

Our range of products now covered most situations where sound attenuation was required. Production was good the staff were good this is what paradise must be like. Unlike the hell we'd experienced at times through our development. The shares in the company were split equally between Jack and myself. He decided to give the majority of his to Julian, retaining a small portion for himself. This was fine by me Julian was now a major part of the company and being younger than me was the future.

The premises which were rented, we were finding too small, we need to move and preferably purchase larger ones. When things are going badly in any situation fate has an acknowledged tendency to compound the situation further. Similarly, when things are going well you can't put a foot wrong, fate would now prove that philosophy. We were willing to consider property within a few miles of our current one. Why do that when the ideal one has just come on the market on the other side of the road. This was the ex-canteen of a large engineering company. It was a single storey building with a large area suitable for manufacturing and excellent office accommodation. With gated access leading into a large, concreted parking and loading area, able to accommodate the largest vehicles. There was also enough area to allow for expansion should we in future need it. Hold on my boy, don't get carried away. So, buy it we did.

With the move we decided to close the ceiling side of the business. The revenue they provided represented only a small percentage of the overall business. The company was originally formed to supply acoustic insulation. The ceilings were introduced when the insulation side of the business was proving difficult. Their worth was immeasurable they had saved the company from folding. The origin for forming the company was now proving its worth and that is where our focus had to be.

CHAPTER NINETEEN

And now the End is Near

Those words seem familiar. We very soon after moving we employed two new women in the office, one over credit control, the other as assistant to Kath. A new man Peter joined us on the sales side he had held a senior position in the glass fibre industry and had taken early retirement. With his experience we hoped he would prove to be a valuable employee, and so it proved. The manufacturing team of Alex, Mathew (Kath's youngest son who had joined us twelve months previous), Sid and Ryan were excellent. Looks like I can spend my time now on some Caribbean beach and obviously Julian thought the same.

He broached the subject asking how would I feel, if he bought my shares, and I could pass into oblivion, I must say I hadn't thought or considered it; indeed, my only thought and consideration was how could the company manage without me. How delusional can you be, thank you I'll accept it, not quite. He obviously thought new blood was needed best to get rid of the old fart. It did come as a surprise not an unpleasant one, but one requiring a little thought. Acoustically was still a new product and its potential was considerable. Had I still the prerequisites of drive, enthusiasm, determination, in the abundance required to sell and promote the products in the way I always had? The never give up, that never say die attitude. I think so. Think! There should be no think about it. If there's any doubt, you have the answer. So, the Caribbean beach here I come.

Jack decided to sell his holding as well. His involvement in recent years had been less. So, after twenty years the company passed to a new broom, or should I say the ownership did. The company was on a very good footing, with an excellent team throughout. I decided to be just another employee for another twelve months. Well, you can't keep a good'n down, I tell myself. After twenty years at the helm, the first ten of which had been very stressful, the remaining less so. Certainly not to be equated though with lying on a Caribbean beach. I enjoyed my last twelve months as one of the gang I put my input in, but operated in a more relaxed mode, not having that little something at the back of your brain known as responsibility. I'd been there and worn the tee shirt and passed it on with the invitation of be my guest.

As I mentioned previously I had originally no ambition to have my own company, circumstances fell that way and I took the opportunity. I never had a desire to be in charge or give orders. I could take them willingly, as long as the ones who gave them, I had respect for, and luckily throughout my working life that had been so. I'd had twenty years experiencing stress, pressure, worry, excitement, anticipation, satisfaction, euphoria I think that's a reasonable selection. I had a very good co-director and friend in Jack, whose integrity, steadfastness and backing, I greatly value and without whom we would not be celebrating a successful company.

And so, the day came I offered my au revoir dried my eyes and went to the pub. I enjoyed a final bash with colleagues past and present in my local a week later. I was fifty-eight was I finished washed up not quite. I'd heard of rehab or courses for retirees who retired from a stressful job and needed help to adjust to post-retirement life. Obviously, my job wasn't stressful enough. I had a phone call from a friend in my first week of wondering what the hell to do. Do you fancy a trip to my cousin's brewery in York next week? How long do you need me to consider it I ask, say no more, if I'd only known, I should have retired at eighteen if this is indicative of retirement, unfortunately it wasn't. Although I adjusted reasonably well, I still had a slight restlessness for the day to day involvement the ducking and diving and the other experiences of business and a selling career. You can't turn off immediately.

Julian came to the rescue. He had been on a brewery tour of a quite recently opened microbrewery. The owner who was an ex-engineer had started the brewery twelve months previous. Julian praised his beer but thought he needed assistance with the marketing. (Are my friends and colleagues kindly guiding me to a career in the brewing industry?) Give him a ring he advises, so ring him I did. Rob was a nice guy who'd brewed beer as a hobby for many years. When he was made redundant and with the suggestion of his friends who obviously appreciated his tipple, he decided to try his luck full time. This rings a bell somewhere, with a similar situation some twenty years before. He supplied a number of pubs, but certainly needed more. He openly admitted selling and marketing was not his forte, plus the brewing and the running of the brewery left him little time for the selling. We agreed I would be paid just commission on every keg I sold to new outlets and on repeat orders, plus expenses for my petrol. I would work how many and whatever days I chose. This was a new challenge for me, and it looked an enjoyable one. My only experience with beer was simply drinking it, after all what else was there to do with it, well I was going to find out. The job appealed, I was doing it not for the money, but for the empathy I shared with Rob having experienced his situation, and the challenge of a new venture in a new trade.

The first thing that was obvious was he had no literature and the pump clips he supplied to fit on the beer pumps of pubs selling his beer were hand-drawn. The clips are the first thing that any prospective drinker sees. They looked amateur and would certainly not tempt any thirsty punter. I offered to get new literature and pump clips designed and printed with a new logo. I would loan the money and he could pay me back over the next year. I would get these done at the studio we used at the company, sorry, that's my old company. I couldn't start selling until I had these, as they were the tools of the trade.

On Monday nights I played indoor tennis with four mates. On our way to the centre I was telling them about how my new venture was going and having the literature and clips made. 'How much will that cost you?' they enquired, 'I think around £500,' I suggested. Richard, one of the four had business dealings with the new owner of a quite large local brewery who had a number of pubs in the area. He had bought this because the local he drank in was one of these, and he liked the beer. Well you sometimes have got to do these things. Richard suggested after tennis we should go to this pub and he would introduce me to this associate, as now I had so much in common with him, so we did, and he introduced me.

'This is a friend of mine; he's just got an interest in a local microbrewery.'

'O yes which brewery is that,' and I told him the name.

'Never heard of it and they are a f_ _ _ _ _ g nuisance these microbreweries, they keep nicking orders from us. I'd only had the brewery for six months and I had to put another million pounds in it.' He said with a slight nonchalant gesture of his hand.

And at that point our common interest ended.

'Well, your £500 is going to go a long way,' was one of the many sympathetic outpourings. That's after they'd all pulled themselves together from there uncontrolled amusement.

I told Rob the story hoping he didn't want a million and reassuring him the £500 was all he needed. The leaflets and the clips arrived, I was pleased with them and so was Rob. The harmonising design of the single page leaflet and pump clips was excellent, the pump clips stood out with a design that was very recognisable and would be equal if not superior to any they were next to on a bar.

Fully armed I had now no excuses and so set off for the first time ever of going into a pub with no intention of drinking. I decided to work one day a week calling on pubs, and one day inside phoning. They were really half days from 12am opening time to 4pm. The reception I received from the landlords on the whole was welcoming after all that was part of their job. It was a learning curve. The majority if they were allowed to, would buy a keg the problem was a large percentage could not. They were tied to purchase all beer and spirits from the pub company or the brewery owning the pub. Some were allowed to buy one guest beer from another source. Our prices were considerably lower than their official source of supply. If it was a free house of which there were very few they could buy from where they liked. The tied houses would slip one in as they would refer to placing an order outside their authorised supplier. They would do this if they knew the local manager wasn't due to call or they weren't having an inspection.

I would receive a phone call from a landlord asking me to get down quickly and pick up the kegs usually empty, as an inspection was due, or a manager was calling. Some of the longer serving landlords would not be quite as fazed with this situation either knowing the manager well, combined with a successful pub with a good turnover. They were given a little more leeway but only so far. It was a far cry in every way from the selling and promotion of my old company. I was doing this for pleasure but with the incentive and aim to help the brewery grow. This I did, increasing the number of pubs sold to, and widening the area covered.

After nearly three years I decided to take my second and final retirement. The job had fulfilled my innate desire for the cut and thrust and involvement in sales and promotion and the growing of a company. I enjoy a satisfaction that my involvement contributed to the success it is today. A couple of years after I left Rob bought a pub which had been closed for a number of years. He extended this and moved the brewery into the new premises. The success of this is down to his and his families hard work and the quality of his product that is his beer, and that is amply displayed by the fact he doesn't sell food, only beer, oh sorry, and spirits. How many pubs do you know who only do that? I have been trying for a number of years to persuade Wendy his dear wife to sell pork pies. She will not hear of it. As soon as I see her and before I can an even say hello, she greats me with 'Don't mention pork pies.' I have achieved a reasonable amount of success in my career, and faced many challenges, but whatever they were, they will pale into insignificance if I can persuade her to sell pork pies. His two sons are now involved with the brewery and pub, so hopefully its longevity is secured.

It was eighteen years ago when I got involved and had the pump clips designed and made. They are the same design today and now well-known and recognised. It was £500 well spent, I wonder if that million was so, and if its necessity can still be seen today.

Although my job with the brewery had been part-time, after forty-six years I finally retired. Now with nothing to do and nowhere to go won't someone listen to my tale of woe, not quite true, I did have some where to go. Twelve months previous we had bought a property in Cyprus, where we spent four enjoyable months every year for the next thirteen years. We made many expat friends; a number have stayed with us on their annual visit to the old country. The visit of the last ones two years ago made a connection by coincidence with an event that had happened fifty-eight years previous which you will recall. I picked them up from the airport, after leaving us they were staying a couple of nights in a hotel in the Pennines I promised to run them there being only fifty minutes away. They spent three days with us and on the fourth we set off to fulfil my promise.

Although it was relatively close, and I had travelled extensively in my career I didn't know the area particularly well. The road which the hotel was on had quite a steep gradient climbing into the hills. Though I did not know the road it had somehow a vague remembrance certainly a case of déjà vu. We reach the hotel and very impressive it was. I parked and we made our way to the reception. Our friends booked in and the young man on reception directed us into the lounge. We were staying for lunch and welcomed a little wetting of the whistle before doing so. My wife asked if I would take something back to the car. On re-entering I notice the name of the licensee over the door and therefore possibly the owner. The name was vaguely familiar. I enquired with the young man on reception if the licensee was also the owner. He confirmed he was and he was his grandfather. 'Did he once own a night club in Bolton?' I asked. He wasn't sure but thought he did. If it was so he possibly knew and was a friend of my father I told him. 'He has an apartment here I call him if you want,' and so he did. 'He'll be down shortly.'

I returned to the lounge and after five minutes this elderly gentleman with the dress and demeanour denying his years approached us.

'So, what have you got to tell me?' he asks.

'Did you own a nightclub in the early sixties in Bolton?'

'Yes.'

'I think you knew my father. He was the one who supplied your drinks and was prosecuted for drinking after hours on your opening night.'

'What was his name?' he enquires.

'Eddie Williams.'

He turns slightly away walks a couple of steps and turns with his hands covering his face.

'Oh my god,' he exclaims

I introduce myself and my wife and explained our presence here. He provides us with a little history of when he bought the place in the sixties and when it opened in 1968. And the penny dropped!

'We came to your opening it was the year we were married. We came with my folks whom you'd invited.' And so, with a fifty year span my case of déjà vu was correct.

Although this experience had no direct connection with my business it had a slight indirect one. When he had first approached us, his face had a slight familiarity. I had last seen him fifty years ago. I was sure I could not have remembered him from then. A couple of days later the second penny dropped. The premises we had moved to after the gatehouse we negotiated with the agent of the owner, who I'd also seen on a few other occasions. They had the same surname and of course features well did you ever what a big coincidence in a small world.

CHAPTER TWENTY

To Summate

And what of the old company? This year 2021 I can say with a little pride and a lot of pleasure it will celebrate its fortieth year. It has grown much more and even without me. It has extended its range to include products to address sound absorption not just stopping the transmission of sound as in my day. They agreed a management buyout from Julian some years ago. This included Kath the longest serving employee of thirty-eight years, a much-deserved reward, and Alex now the MD who joined as a temporary job before going to college, some temporary job, and I am pleased to say it is in good hands,

It seems a long way from the time I sat in the office of the largest ceiling contractor in the northwest between Christmas and New Year in 1980, hoping they would back me in forming a company with my new business venture. They had everything I had nothing my future on a knife edge, and within forty years I have everything that I want, within reason, and they have nothing. They ceased trading many years ago. Not long after this when Jack and I had just decided to form the company I was phoned by the second largest ceiling contractor in the northwest and offered a rep's job. I explained my new venture and thanked them. They went bankrupt many years ago. What does this tell you? Apart from what the hell was I thinking of in forming a company, do your own thing back yourself, well in my case with Jack's help.

When we first started the company as I have previously mentioned ceiling contractors were a main outlet for our business. Throughout the north and northeast, I knew many, especially in the northwest. I wouldn't be sure how many there were forty years ago in the northwest, but it was a considerable amount. Of those companies I am aware now of only two that are still in business. The same would apply to the rest of the north probably counting on one hand those still trading from that period. The building game can be a precarious business especially for subcontractors. There will be a number of reasons why there are so few of that era left but I would put financial failure top of the list.

There are approximately on average 650,000startup companies per year in the UK. That seems quite a staggering amount. In the first year 20% fail, 30% in the second, 60% in the third. Don't let me put you off. So, what makes a successful company? There are many people more able and qualified and far more successful than I to answer that question. But with the company I helped to start that is now forty years old and twenty of the formative years I was involved I have a few ideas.

Hard work, good staff, and a product that people want, are a good start. A product they want, you would think was obvious, allow me to clarify. That is a product they want, not what you think they want. *Forbes* business magazine reported in May 2019. The number one reason why start ups fail is 'no market need.' I refer back to Insuleeze the product we brought out and won the prize for, but very few orders. It wasn't quite as black and white with Insuleeze there were a few other factors, but the principle applied. Many products have been brought out with the enthusiasm, belief, integrity of the producer and failed because they have not been fully researched or thought through. Just check on the internet, the list is near endless. The two points I have mentioned I believe are fundamental, but they are only part of the package. They in themselves do not guarantee success. Confidence in your ability is a must. That is not confidence to run a business but confidence in your chosen profession. Be it a salesman, an engineer, a joiner, a welder, a plumber or whatever it may be. You can learn and get advice on how to run a business. By the time you are considering that you should know how good you are at your profession.

Get a good accountant. Your interest in forming a company is to promote and sell your product your skill your services. It is not to become a financial wizard at least not at the outset. Unless of course your intended company is in financial services. The accountancy or financial side is in most cases a bugbear or an unavoidable necessity, one that interrupts your main purpose. But it is a fundamental part of your business possibly 50%, it certainly is if things go wrong, hence the need for a good accountant, one who can offer guidance and advice. When we formed the company, we had two directors, me on sales, marketing and production, and Jack over the accounts. He dealt with the day-to-day accountancy, the cash flow the planning and the bank. This relieved me of the accounting side, other than you may recall when I had to get £15,000, into the bank by 1pm. You're never completely without involvement.

Sufficient funds and cash flow, lack of these are one of the main reasons for business failure. Of course, overdrafts are a large part of these, and collateral is what is needed to obtain and sustain them. Many director's and partner's houses used as collateral have been lost when company failure has occurred.

A good product and pride in what you sell or produce, if you haven't got it pack in, you will be found out. You will survive for a certain amount of time but that is all. Sales and marketing, if you don't sell you don't survive. If you can't or don't like selling get someone who can and does. A good salesman can make or save a company, and I speak from personal experience, not boasting of course. I am not referring to my own company although I hope I had some influence with that, but a previous one which I was informed I saved from going under.

Trust is paramount both with your co-directors and they with you, without it you're on shaky ground. It is not just trust in honesty it is trust in the contribution of work that each put into the company. This can be more critical if there are only two directors or partners in the company. In time it becomes apparent if one is contributing more than the other. It could be one has more ambition one is more laid back; their ideas or strategy may clash; one may have a stronger personality. It is only once the company is up and

running that these cracks or differences often appear. If two have worked together previously it is an advantage but not the panacea for all ills. I liken it to friends or couples who have known each other for years and get on fine. Then they come and stay with you in your house for two or three weeks. All may be fine, and then again all may be not.

Make sure if you're considering going into partnership you analyse and give careful thought to your prospective partner. Do not be blinded by the excitement and anticipation of having your own company or being your own boss.

There's a line from the song 'I wish I were in love again,' by Rogers & Hart, which is nothing to do with business, well not intended to be but appropriate, the sleepless nights, the daily fights, the quick toboggan when you reach the heights' sums it up quite well. It can be a long gruelling process. If successful it can be satisfying, and very rewarding both financially and in achievement. If not in extremes a shotgun has been known to be the answer.

If you are tempted to do it and feel you have something to offer that people want (and make sure that they do) don't be put off by the fear of the pitfalls. If you have researched, covered all aspects, got sufficient capital and have confidence, go for it. Be positive companies do not succeed with negativity. That does not mean you do not ever hesitate about decisions or you do not have doubts, or you don't make mistakes, but these are overridden by a vision to go forward. Set your aim of where you want to go, what you want to achieve. Let these be the driving force and the day to day running or problems you face, you will cut through, they will not cling you will throw them off. If you have no or little aim, problems will be magnified and appear more intense. The purpose of your business is not to manufacture or produce problems it is to manufacture and produce whatever is its founding purpose. Businesses have two gears forward and reverse, make sure you engage the right one.

My father was a salesman, I have been a salesman my son is now a salesman. My father's patch was between Bolton, Salford and Manchester, mine was between Bolton, London and Glasgow, my sons is between Gdansk, Hong Kong and Miami. Well, when it's in the blood that's progress. I have enjoyed my career and working life, if you don't it must be hell, and what a waste of fifty or so years. I've made mistakes, I wish in a way I'd also had more ambition from an earlier age. Overall, I'm quite satisfied with my working life it has afforded me a pleasant retirement. Is there anything I would have changed? Certainly, one thing, I would have made sure my office when we were in the mill was fully soundproofed to stop the radio blasting through interrupting my phone calls. But then I would have had to find someone who could do it, and who also knew what they were doing.

Acnowledgments

In memory of Jack Donnelly without whom this book would not have been written

I would like to offer my thanks to the following. Pete Guttridge, whose help and encouragement at the beginning has now been rewarded. Brian Evans, whose support and endorsement was instrumental in me publishing the book. Julian Donnelly, whose suggestions and corrections were necessary.